BRITISH RAILCARS

1900 TO 1950

David Jenkinson & Barry C. Lane

TRANSPORT
Atlantic
PUBLISHERS

PREFACE

The gestation of this work has been complex. Some ten years or so ago, I wrote a general review of British Railway Carriages in the first half of the 20th Century in which I covered as much variety as possible within the generous, but still limited space available. At a later date, I began to expand some themes for the benefit of modelmakers and one or two of them appeared in *Modellers' Backtrack* (MBT), a magazine which I introduced when I was in charge of Atlantic Transport Publishers. Less than four years later, personal health circumstances forced me to merge MBT with its parent BACKTRACK at a new monthly frequency and to hand over control of Atlantic to a new owners. At the same time, the idea of a more extended treatment of selected carriage themes was felt to be worth pursuing in the new monthly BACKTRACK and I was therefore asked if I could prepare a few topics. This was duly done and at the time of writing (late 1995) some of these have begun to appear.

'Railcars' was one such theme — until it became clear that the material which was accumulating was far too much for even a multi-part article, at which point, a second idea began to form. The demise of MBT was much regretted by many of Atlantic's readers who liked the more detailed approach to selected aspects of the prototype railways which had been its particular metier. It thus seemed possible that there was a case for an occasional publication in the style of BACKTRACK whose aim would be to fill the sort of gap left by the demise of MBT. This work is a consequence of that re-thinking and I am delighted that the new owner of Atlantic has agreed to offer it as the 'first fruit' of what we all hope may soon be a flourishing new plant on which may be cultivated a series of appropriate themes — by no means all carriage-based.

I should, however, point out that though written by a modelmaker (and, to some extent, inspired by the needs of the modelmaking fraternity), this is *not* a modelmaking book as such. True, I have included a multiplicity of pictures and a number of drawings which I hope modellers will find useful, but my main purpose has been to try and place a particular and somewhat specialised theme into the broader perspective of railway history. I would therefore hope that it will be of equal if not greater interest to the general reader. This book is, therefore, slightly experimental in concept and I am sure that both I and the publisher will appreciate any comments which readers may care to send.

Although the survey ranges far and wide, I do not claim to have included every British railcar which ever existed before the 1950s, though I think I may have trapped most of them! Nor have I been able to illustrate every variety mentioned — space would simply not permit this. I have, however, tried to give as good a spread as possible and I have at least seen pictures of every type described. This book, therefore, is essentially a retrospective overview and does not stand substitute for the more detailed accounts in print which cover quite a number of aspects in greater detail. Those known to me are included in the brief bibliography at the end and I have no doubt that readers who would like to explore this fascinating story in more depth will find much value therein and may well discover further references too which I have not seen.

In some ways the study is somewhat uneven, this being a reflection of the variability and quality of available sources — and steam inevitably dominates if only because of its greater variety of visible variants during the period in question; but I hope this will not reduce its interest as a general review of developing ideas. And here, I should state that my study is confined to mainland Britain only. This is not to dismiss the unique Ulster contribution; rather, it recognises the fact that in a recent issue of BACKTRACK (Volume 9, No.11), the Northern Irish story was covered in some detail. To repeat it here would seem superfluous and, of course, the Irish Republic ceased to be 'British', in the literal sense of the word, after the post-World War I partition.

Finally, I must, as always, thank those who have helped. In particular, in this case, I must single out my good friend Barry Lane. Not only has he designed the whole work to his usual high standard but he is also personally responsible for discovering (and making suitable for reproduction) the fine colour image on the front cover. Add to this his vital role in terms of supplying additional material and helping determine the content and structure of the book and the reason for his name appearing on the cover as well as mine will be obvious. Likewise, I am indebted to John Edgington for providing many fine views from his own private collection and to Nick Campling for some fine drawings and pictures of LNER and constituent railcars. Thanks go too to my former colleagues at the National Railway Museum for placing the museum's photographic files at my disposal. Last, but certainly not least, sincere thanks go to Dick Riley for not only providing the fine colour image on the rear cover, but also for his eleventh hour efforts to discover and provide b/w views of some of the rarer railcar types which the 'home team' had been unable to track down. All known authorship of pictures is credited in the captions (many are anonymous, however) and I extend apologies in advance if any have been wrongly attributed through ignorance on my part. If there be such instances, perhaps the publisher could be advised accordingly.

David Jenkinson
Raskelf, North Yorkshire
January 1996

Prepared and produced by the Pendragon Partnership on behalf of Atlantic Transport Publishers, Trevithick House, West End, Penryn, Cornwall, TR10 8HE. All rights reserved

Design/Artwork by Barry C. Lane, Sutton-in-Craven

Printed by The Amadeus Press Ltd, Huddersfield, West Yorkshire

British Cataloguing-in-Publication Data: a catalogue reference for this book is held by the British Library

ISBN No. 0 906899 64 8

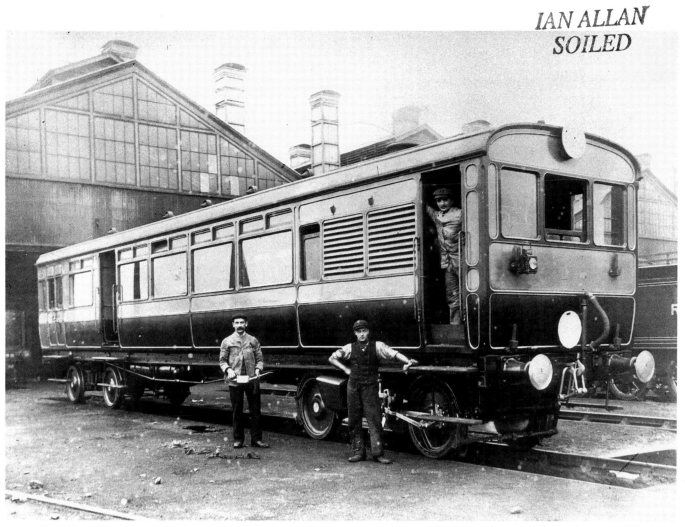

Dugald Drummond of the London & South Western Railway was the first British engineer to tackle the steam railcar seriously. After a few earlier experiments, which began in 1902, the type illustrated here became his 'standard' design. This is No.5 at Eastleigh c.1910 — see also Chapter 2. (R. C. Riley collection)

CONTENTS

Chapter 1	**The Role and Nature of the Railcar**	4
Chapter 2	**The Rise and Fall of the First Steam Railcars**	9
	The rigid framed steam railcar	13
	The articulated steam railcar	21
Chapter 3	**Enter Internal Combustion**	36
Chapter 4	**A Second Chance for Steam**	46
Chapter 5	**The Triumph of the Diesel**	68
	Bibliography	81

The steam powered railcar was usually the first serious attempt to make some form of economy. Many varied types were introduced but this Furness Railway design of 1905 is a good example to offer at this stage, largely because, and somewhat unusually, it also operated with a purpose built trailer car. (Pendragon Collection)

Chapter One

THE ROLE AND NATURE OF THE RAILCAR

SINCE THE TURN OF THE CENTURY, the railways have been striving to find some sort of solution to the increasing problems of road competition and during the early 20th Century, in terms of passenger travel in a more purely urban context, the electrification of routes often helped in face of the problems caused by the new electric tramway and, later, motor bus competition. Likewise, higher speed and improved amenity generally served to maintain the viability of long distance operations. But the middle ground (ie intermediate distance routes) was often a problem and, interestingly, is still perhaps the major area where the modern railway is hardest pressed to compete. In more recent days, of course, a regular solution has often been to abandon the unequal struggle and close the service, letting the road competitor take over, if he can; but far too often in recent years, he too has been found wanting — deregulated buses for example!

Now before I go further, let it be made clear that I do not believe that the railway has a divine right to take preference over roads; the two should, ideally, live in harmony, each playing to and feeding from the relative strengths of the other. But in the curiously unregulated nature of *public* transport which has been the bane of this nation since early Victorian times, things have never been that simple. We have never had an overall public transport policy and yet the private railways in their pre-1948 form were, arguably more than all other institutions, the key factor in creating a strong public perception that there ought to be a form of minimal public service *as a matter of right*. I therefore hold it to their eternal credit that most of our old private companies regularly managed to provide such a service from a purely commercial base. Nevertheless, during this century it has become clear that such problems as existed

before the first world war were as nothing compared with those which began to emerge during the inter-war era and have continued ever since.

The nature of the problem is basically twofold, and even though I accept the limitations of trying to analyse a complex situation in such a simple way, I feel that it is helpful to try to reduce matters to fundamental components. On this basis, the first issue was the search for a cheaper way of operating the quieter routes, while the second was the problem of how to provide some sort of service for those who have no other choice, especially as an ever increasing number of the population no longer use railways at all. Of the two, the latter is probably the more dominant; but in the last analysis, the bottom line will be and always has been one of costs, and to make any significant reduction in this area means some form of passenger carrying facility which is cheaper both to build and operate than a conventional locomotive and train. Events were to show that whatever the precise technology, a form of self-propulsion was the answer.

There is nothing particularly revolutionary in this appraisal — it has been known for the best part of 100 years — but in purely British terms it took the form of four distinct phases of evolution, the last of which culminated in the Diesel multiple unit revolution of the 1950s and all that followed since. I am even inclined to suggest that the British manifestation of what in time became an international type of solution, may never have happened in the form which it did but for the historic experience of the pre-1948 private companies; so it is the primary purpose of this survey to outline the evolution of this story. It is a fascinating tale and I am happy to leave readers to draw their own conclusion as to its long term significance.

However, at this stage, I must re-iterate that the vital concept is 'self-propelled' — ie not dependent on an outside source of tractive power. Thus, this review is not concerned with the electric multiple unit which, wherever the high infrastructure costs of the external traction supply can be justified, has often proven itself the ideal solution to more densely trafficked routes. Our concern here, at the risk of over-repetition, is the middle ground in which context, the infrastructure costs of any form of fixed electrification have usually ruled it out as a solution.

Self-propulsion can take on a considerable variety of cosmetic external forms — in which lies much of its undoubted fascination — but in both the technological and historical sense, the railway industry has usually adopted one of but two 'prime movers': steam and internal combustion. There were, it is true, a few not very successful experiments with battery electric propulsion but, as with those which have been tried thus far on the roads (written in 1995), the main stumbling block seems always to have been the problem of battery storage both in terms of weight and bulk. I do not, therefore, propose to cover this part of the subject since it has not really been of long-term significance. The future, of course, may be different. . .

So what, exactly, constitutes a self-propelled 'railcar'? Setting aside the obvious fact that it should contain *within itself* the means of propulsion as well as seats for the passengers, I feel it is important to emphasise that the design should represent an 'integrated concept'. I say this because there were some examples (the former Lancashire and Yorkshire Railway steam railmotors spring immediately to mind) where the 'locomotive' part was quite separate from the passenger carrying portion in the purely technical sense. But neither could function independently of the other — and that is the important distinction which will govern this survey. Most of them, on this definition, were 'single unit' in conceptual terms, even if they were actually two separate physical parts (ie one 'prime mover' and a separate passenger-carrying part). On this basis, the very few exceptions can readily be dealt with as they arise.

An associated problem which also needs to be faced is one of terminology. In the British context there were several words or phrases which, historically, were used by railway companies, such as 'motor train' (even if steam-powered!), 'railmotors' (same caveat!), 'steam railmotors' (interesting, that one!), 'railcars' and so-forth. No doubt, at the time, everybody knew what was meant but viewed from a longer distance, they can be confusing. I should, therefore, perhaps, make it clear that I shall use the word 'railcar' somewhat indiscriminately to cover all self-propelled units to be described, be they integral or made up of powered and non-powered units, the vital point being that the latter should be incapable of operation without their design partner. Not only is 'railcar', on the whole, the most appropriate word to define such a concept, but it avoids the linguistic complication which any other word might cause, even though I shall mention some other terms from time to time.

All of which suggests that I should also define the term 'trailer' car, an expression which will often appear in these pages. In essence, a trailer car was a vehicle which had no self-contained means of propulsion, albeit that many were built, if required, so as to be capable of being adapted to accept controls for the driver via some form of remote control apparatus. They could therefore be found in association either with a self-propelled railcar or with a separate locomotive — sometimes either — and herein lies their difference from what was often called the 'trailer portion' (ie the non-powered element) of an integrally designed railcar unit. The fact that many railcars were subsequently converted to a form of non-powered 'trailer' which *could* be operated with a conventional locomotive need not concern us too much, being, thankfully, outwith the terms of reference of this survey. But mention of conventional locomotives does suggest that some readers might like to know where stands the so-called 'Push & Pull' solution in this analysis.

This latter idea was a variant of the more conventional system in that the locomotive (albeit adapted for operation from the opposite end of a so-called 'driving trailer' car when the

As well as company-inspired offerings, some steam railcars were developed by independent manufacturers in the hope that the railways would take an interest. This typical example, a small railcar built by Ganz of Budapest and re-erected by Brush of Loughborough (where it was photographed on 2nd June 1905), was intended to be manufactured under licence by the Peebles Steam Railcar Co. It was tried on the Midland, but although this type (or others to similar design) was to become quite widespread in Europe, it did not seem to find favour in Britain (NRM Collection)

'Push-Pull' was often a better eventual solution than the steam railcar, but few railways offered purpose built examples, most of them preferring to use modified 'ordinary' stock. The London and South Western Railway was one exception and Dugald Drummond's purpose-built 1906 follow-on to his railcar designs covered in Chapter 2 must serve as sole representative of a concept only marginally relevant to this survey. It also illustrates the interior — reasonably typical of many purpose built railcar designs of the time as well and not always renowned for comfort! (NRM Collection — 2)

locomotive was pushing) was also capable of being detached from the trailer and used independently in a fully conventional manner whenever required. This did not give the complete 'Push-Pull' ensemble the self-contained and integral nature of the railcar so I have excluded it, save for references to its role in relation to those ideas which it sometimes (often?) replaced. During the 'traditional' steam railway era, 'Push-Pull' was an operation almost entirely confined to the passenger workings in the 'middle ground' with which this survey is mainly concerned and was undoubtedly instrumental in terms of shortening the working life of many (most?) railcars. Widely practiced until the end of steam, it was an idea which, interestingly, has recently been revived in full measure in our modern day (for rather different reasons) with anything up to ten or more coaches now being 'pushed' by the locomotive for hundreds of miles along our main lines at up to 140mph.

So, having established the essential parameters, it is now possible to set the history of the British railcar into perspective. Unsurprisingly, it began with steam at the turn of the century when many railways came up with a whole variety of lightweight steam powered units, often of considerable ingenuity. Not much later, a second idea began to emerge in the form of early experiments with the then quite new internal combustion engine. Although most of these ideas (of either type) came to nought, the 'steam plus internal combustion' cycle was then repeated (mostly during the 1930s) in rather more sophisticated form. These four separate technical phases, overlapping in time to some extent, culminated in the first truly nationwide solution in the form of the first generation BR standard diesel multiple units (DMUs) of the 1950s. It is the four antecedent phases of this DMU revolution which form the remaining part of this review.

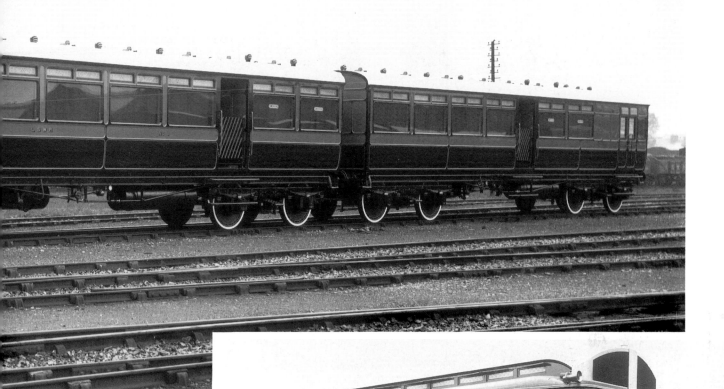

North Eastern petrol railcar No.3768 (see also Chapter 3), though intended purely for inspection purposes, was not too untypical of the early century experiments with internal combustion and had a more railway-like character than many.
(T. J. Edgington Collection)

Several commercial motor firms experimented with rail vehicles during the period under survey. Most of the more significant ventures are covered in Chapters 3 and 5 but little seems to be on record about this neat example from the Daimler company, seen here at Kenilworth on the old London and North Western Railway. The original picture suggests a pre-1914 date but the car is very reminiscent of the better tramcar practice of the inter-war years. Whatever, it is not untypical of the kind of ideas which were being evaluated as alternatives to steam.
(F. W. Shuttleworth Collection)

The 'second coming' of steam propulsion was dominated by Sentinel railcars, particularly on the London and North Eastern Railway — see Chapter 4. This attractive view from the 1930s shows an unidentified example on just the sort of duty for which the type was designed: intermediate workings on cross-country lines. The location is near Goathland on the old NER Whitby to Pickering route — better known these days as the North Yorkshire Moors Railway. (LNER Official)

The best answer, at least in pre-BR days, was probably offered by the GWR with its stylish diesel railcars — Chapter 5. This 1952 view shows No.W15W at Welford Park on the Newbury to Lambourn branch, yet again a suitably appropriate location for such a vehicle. (M. W. Earley — courtesy NRM)

Chapter Two

THE RISE AND FALL OF THE FIRST STEAM RAILCARS

I**T WAS ENTIRELY PREDICTABLE** that when the pre-group companies began to consider the new style of road competition in areas where full scale electrification and its concomitant intensive services was not an option, they turned to some form of 'modified' version of the conventional steam train; unsurprisingly, the first phase in the appraisal usually resulted in that uniquely Edwardian phenomenon, the steam railcar — or steam railmotor as it was often called.

This was always achieved by means of a self-propelled single unit which embodied a combination of a small locomotive portion with a passenger carrying area. Two alternatives were assayed: the 'rigid' railcar wherein the locomotive part was mounted on the same frame as the passenger portion and the rather more sophisticated 'articulated' option in which the powered end, though usually semi-permanently attached to the carriage end, could pivot independently.

In most cases, the rigid type usually displayed an outward form in which the engine part was fully integrated with the carriage bodywork — ie (more or less) totally concealed from view — while the articulated type most commonly had an engine part fully exposed to view and bearing the visible lineaments of a conventional steam locomotive. There were exceptions to this general state of affairs (more particularly in the articulated type) and the rigid type was to enjoy an approximate 2:1 superiority overall. But what was really surprising was that although no fewer than 21 different railways tackled the problem between 1902 and 1911, producing almost 200 examples of the genre in the process, only four companies built them in

double figure quantities and of these, the GWR accounted for almost exactly half the total built. The appended Table gives further details, from which it can be seen that the GWR and LSWR favoured 'concealed' styling, whereas the LYR and TVR went for the alternative mode.

Curiously, however — and discounting a few rather weird and impracticable 19th Century ideas — the first genuine railcar design was devised in 1902 by the formidable Dugald Drummond of the LSWR for the joint LSWR/LB&SCR service between Southsea and Fratton. Although the GWR borrowed one later and reported quite favourably on it, they were actually feeble machines with insufficient steam raising power to keep going when fully loaded. Thus, they unwittingly pioneered not only the railcar type but accurately predicted its principal subsequent failing, no matter who built it, for what purpose or to what design.

The need to rebuild the engine portion of Drummond's pioneer cars changed what had been a neat and unobtrusive design into one of surpassing ugliness as far as the 'business end' was concerned — 'loutish' as one writer aptly put it! However, in revised form they gave nearly twenty years service — better than many. But they did not typify the subsequent British steam railcars which are perhaps best considered in terms of basic structural form, starting with the 'rigid frame' type. Drummond's original cars were of this type, of course, but in the event, they turned out to be the only rigid steam railcars to display an exposed locomotive portion — the rest had the 'works' well and truly concealed in what was, in effect, a continuation of the carriage portion.

PURPOSE BUILT STEAM RAILCARS: 1902-11									
		Rigid style			Articulated style			Grand	
Date	Company	Open loco	Enclosed loco	Sub total	Open loco	Enclosed loco	Sub total	Total	
1904-5	Alexandra Docks		2	2				2	* The last British company to introduce the type
1905	Barry		2	2				2	
1911	Cardiff*		2	2				2	
1905	Furness		2	2				2	+ In effect, these cars had an partly enclosed locomotive portion with an external chimney/smokebox door ahead of the concealed portion
1904-5	Great Central		3	3				3	
1905	Great Northern				6		6	6	
1905	GNSR				2		2	2	
1904-5	G&SWR				3		3	3	
1903-8	Great Western		97	97		2	2	99	
1906	IoW Central				1		1	1	
1905	LB&SCR				2+	2+	2+		# These totals relate to the number of carriage portions. In both cases there were spare locomotive units - see text
1905-10	LNWR		7	7				7	
1904-6	LSWR		15	15				15	
1902	LSWR/LB&SC Jt	2		2				2	
1905-11	LYR				17#		17#	17#	
1904	Midland		2	2				2	§ The only British steam railcar with a six-coupled locomotive portion
1905-6	North Staffs				3+		3+	3+	
1906	Port Talbot					1§	1§	1§	
1907	Rhymney				2		2	2	
1904-5	SE&CR				8		8	8	
1903-6	Taff Vale				16#		16#	16#	
	TOTALS	2	132	134	55	8	63	197	

These two crisp official views were obviously taken at the same time and give a very good 'all round' view of Britain's first genuine steam railcar design: Dugald Drummond's pioneer effort for the LSWR/LB&SC joint service between Fratton and Southsea. No.1 was one of a pair built in 1902, but the vertical boiler was too feeble and within a year or so both cars were given a rather less elegant 'locomotive type' boiler.
(SR Official — 2)

In rebuilt form, the Drummond cars were far more effective, aesthetics notwithstanding. This June 1904 view of No.2 (thought to be at Portsmouth) was taken less than a year after reboilering took place in October 1903.. (NRM collection)

GWR Railcar No.17 entered service in April 1904 as the first example of the second production batch (cars 17-28) of the 'matchboard-side' style of car. It was technically regarded as the 'branch' type — ie with extra luggage capacity — though one picture exists showing it in suburban type service at Brentford. It ceased to be a railcar in 1919 but the carriage portion was converted to auto-trailer No.113.
(NRM collection)

Left:
The so-called suburban type of early GWR railcar is represented in this view of car No.7 in rural surroundings at St Agnes, Cornwall at an unknown date during the Edwardian era. It therefore seems, see previous picture, that the operational distinction between the two types was somewhat 'blurred'. Built in 1904, this car was one of the first production series of suburban units (3-14 — see text) and was converted to auto-trailer No.103 in 1915.
(Pendragon Collection)

This view at Shepherds, Cornwall (also on the long since vanished Newquay to Chacewater line — see previous view of No.7) shows car No.24 in service c.1910. It was taken out of service as a railcar in May 1920, becoming auto-trailer No.120.
(Pendragon Collection)

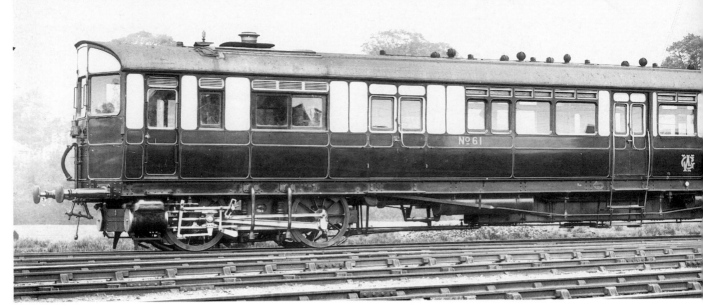

This fine official GWR view shows the second style of railcar panelling as applied to No.61, a so-called 'branch' car built in 1906. It is attached to purpose-built trailer No.34, not to be confused with railcar No.34 of 1905, though built at much the same time to much the same style. In 1905, the GWR began experimenting with small tank engines fitted with 'auto' gear and pairing them with purpose built trailers as an alternative to running the latter with railcars. The engine-plus-trailer combination was, in due course, found the more satisfactory, hence the later conversion of most former railcars into trailer form. Railcar No.61 was thus converted in December 1927 and became trailer No.150. (GWR Official)

GWR Railcar No.63 of the same series as the previous view, seen in 'all lake' livery and thought to be in the Oxford area around the World War I period. Withdrawn as a railcar in 1927, along with No.61 (see previous view) it became trailer No.151. (B. C. Lane Collection)

This interesting view shows a pair of freshly overhauled GWR engine units outside Swindon Works in 1932. They cannot be individually identified nor was it recorded to which railcars they would be allocated. (T. E. Layne from R. C. Riley Collection)

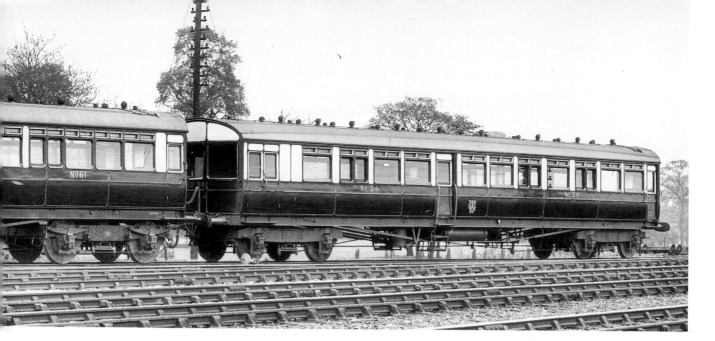

The rigid framed steam railcar

The GWR was not only the 'market leader' (again see Table I), but was also first in the field (1903) after Drummond; and its cars displayed variation in both appearance and design detail. If truth be told, they were not the most elegant looking vehicles by GWR standards, but their sheer numbers, compared with the rest, represented the only truly serious attempt by a major British company to persevere with this particular solution to the fundamental operating problem.

Two types were assayed, the so called 'Suburban' and 'Branch line' types whose nomenclature, even at that early stage, revealed a sort of conceptual uncertainty which was to affect all subsequent steam railcar development. For the record, the suburban variant had no separate luggage compartment, but it was never adequately explained how broadly the same sort of unit could, at one and the same time, be appropriate both for lightly used branch lines and for busy suburban services. However, in the latter environment, it may have been thought that one way to compete with the tramcar was to build a similar type of vehicle (in seating capacity terms) which could traverse the suburbs at frequent intervals and more rapidly than on the public highway. In this regard, it was indeed successful but many later proved themselves incapable of pulling an extra trailer to carry the new customers which their success had generated!

But clearly, the steam railcar fulfilled a more than useful purpose on the GWR — the numbers built reveal that — and this was especially true in country areas where, on average, the branch line type outlived its suburban counterpart by some ten years. By the mid-1930s, they were mostly replaced either by the familiar auto-train (an independent small locomotive working push-pull with one or more trailers) or the new diesel railcars, to be covered later in this survey. It is also worth recalling that most of the GWR steam railcars enjoyed a second, and often lengthy lease of life, when they were rebuilt as auto-trailers.

Fortunately, the GWR cars (including those of the post-1922 constituents of the GWR) have been studied and recorded in some detail as part of the well known pioneering work of the Railway Correspondence and Travel Society in its definitive locomotive history series (see also Bibliography). To repeat this material would, therefore, be unnecessary. But a few general points will not be out of place in this review.

In terms of styling, the GWR cars embodied two principal variants, apart from the two articulated cars (GWR Nos.15/16) which will be considered in the next section. The first to appear displayed a somewhat austere slab sided form with match-board side panels below the waist and whose appearance was

The last GWR steam railcars lasted in until 1935 — a near-30 year life which well exceeded most of the genre, whether from the GWR or elsewhere. This is either No.88 or 98 (more probably the latter) at Southall on the Brentford branch service. Both cars were withdrawn in 1935, No.88 being scrapped and No.98 becoming trailer No.215.
(T. J. Edgington Collection)

quite unlike anything the GWR had hitherto offered in the carriage field. This type of construction seemed to enjoy a brief vogue during early Edwardian years for a few companies (the NER did something rather similar in the locomotive hauled field with equally unmemorable aesthetic appeal), but the GWR never used it save on its railcars. Two 'prototypes' were built in 1903, followed by the main batch in 1904 (Nos.3-14, 17-28) which embodied some minor differences.

Later, the company changed to a more traditionally panelled style which it applied consistently to its largest single group of railcars (Nos.29-99) built 1905-8. However, although thoroughly 'British' in its fundamental approach, the actual panelling detail of these 'second generation' GWR railcars was differently proportioned from that of the contemporary locomotive hauled stock, particularly in its use of a very deep waist panel. This distinctive styling also remained confined to railcars but both forms of railcar 'architecture' remained a unique and distinctive identifying feature of GWR branch-type operations when the bulk of the railcars were later converted to auto-trailers.

Barry Railway Steam Railmotor No.2 was one of a pair built at the Atlas works of the N.B. Loco. Co. in Glasgow in 1905. The neat bodies came from the nearby firm of R. Y. Pickering of Wishaw. The location is not specified but the cars were mostly used on the Vale of Glamorgan line. Withdrawn in 1914, the cars were converted to trailers, No.2 becoming Barry No.178 (later GWR 4303) and in GWR days they were further converted to a gangwayed pair and fitted with the GWR control system.
(E. R. Mountford from R. C. Riley Collection)

It seems from the record that the GWR cars were to be seen throughout the system and some of them initiated new services as well as taking over some or all of the existing traffic. They were not unsuccessful but, as stated, their regular success in attracting extra patronage exceeded their limitations. Thus, a full size locomotive and carriages became viable where previously the traffic did not warrant it. In the GWR case, this regularly took the form of Push-Pull 'Auto' trains, hence the conversion of most railcars to trailer form.

Three of the GWR constituents had offered rigid railcars prior to 1923 — see Table I. In each case a pair of cars was obtained mostly for a specific service and none of them had a particularly long life in railcar form. The two Alexandra Docks cars worked between Caerphilly and Pontypridd for a few years and were differently styled: though both were vaguely similar to the two early Drummond cars (above), No.2 had a clerestory. They lasted until 1911 and 1917.

The Barry and Cardiff Railways each bought a pair of identical twins whose designs, though different from each other, were not dissimilar from those of the GWR itself in style or size. After a short life as railcars, they were converted into trailer cars in 1914 (Barry Railway) and c.1917 (Cardiff Railway) and as such went into GWR stock after the grouping. Interestingly, the Cardiff cars had originally been augmented by a pair of trailer cars and these too were absorbed into the GWR trailer fleet.

It is likely, given that the GWR was so influential, that a number of other companies went into the steam railmotor business by way of imitation; but of those which adopted the rigid enclosed type, most did so on on what looks very much like an experimental basis, judging by the quantities built. All had much in common and some were distinctly stylish, but only the LSWR and LNWR tackled them with any seriousness and even they did not seem wholly convinced.

The fifteen LSWR examples displayed running gear much influenced by the first Drummond machines but the bodywork was 'cleaner' with, apart from the first two, a very neatly enclosed locomotive portion embodying 'coachbuilt' styling.

The first pair of LSWR railcars proper (ie following the two joint cars already considered) were ordered in 1903 and based on experience gained with the earlier cars. They displayed a fully enclosed engine part, encased in a rather severe 'tin tabernacle'. A new number series was started and No.1 is shown here at Hounslow, leaving for Gunnersbury c.1910, a service to which they were transferred in that year after having been tried out in various parts of the LSWR system from 1904, their date of introduction to service. They were withdrawn in 1916. (NRM Collection)

Above: The most numerous group of LSWR railcars was authorised in 1904 and the thirteen examples concerned (Nos.3-15) emerged during 1905-6. They all displayed a much neater 'coachbuilt' style at the powered end and this fine ex-works view shows No.5 when new. After running in and along with No.6, it was sent to Exmouth Junction and operated the Exeter-Honiton shuttle service and later (1908) between Exeter and Topsham. It was withdrawn in November 1916.
(SR Official)

When new, the LSWR railcars were run-in on the Botley to Bishop's Waltham branch and in this view, brand new No.8 is seen on this duty at the latter location. Built in January 1906, it was first allocated to Guildford for the Bordon branch, but by mid-1906, replaced at Guildford by No.10, was sent to join No.2 at Plymouth whence it operated to Turnchapel and St. Budeaux. In 1910 it went to Strawberry Hill for services to Gunnersbury. Like all but three of this series of cars, it was withdrawn in November 1916. In 1919, like all the others, it was converted to a trailer. (Pendragon Collection)

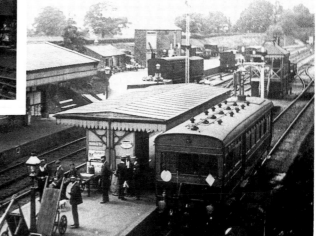

This undated view (but probably c.1906), shows an unidentified LSWR railcar on the usual running-in turn at Brotley, junction for the Bishop's Waltham line. The picture is not totally clear but will be of interest to modellers by virtue of showing the roof top arrangement. (Pendragon Collection)

By contrast, the first two enclosed cars had somewhat uncompromising steel platework at the powered end. All fifteen were usually used in the branch line mode but in 1906 Drummond introduced his own version of the auto-train and the railcars soon went. Only three were left in 1916 and all had gone by 1919. Once again, considerable amplifying detail of these and the LSWR/LB&SCR joint cars has been recorded, this time in D. L. Bradley's four-volume history of LSWR locomotives (see Bibliography).

The LNWR did not espouse the steam railmotor with any great enthusiasm but the few which it did build (six in 1905-7 and a more powerful example with a separate trailer in 1910) were undeniably stylish — probably more so than any others, save perhaps for those of the Furness and Great Central Rail-

ways. All three of these companies seemed to produce a more visually harmonious unit than the otherwise more significant GWR and LSWR examples. Yet again, and this seems to have been typical of most steam railcars, the actual styling involved in all three cases, though typically British, was distinctly different from contemporary locomotive hauled stock. One suspects that 'newness' may have had to be shown to be present in the cosmetic as well as the technical sense!

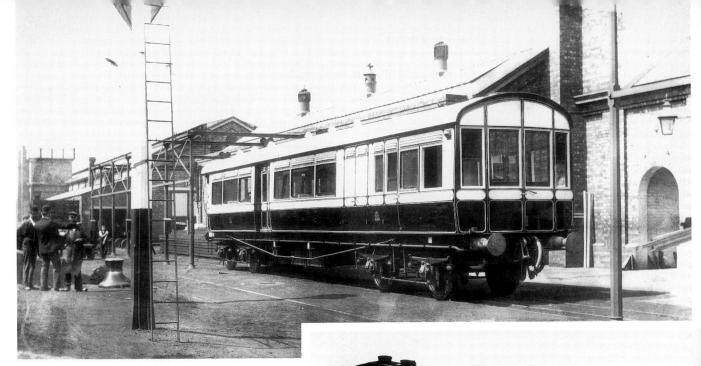

These ex-works views show the opposite sides of Railcars Nos.1 and 3, the handsome LNWR design of 1905. The view taken at Wolverton works shows No.3 mounted on temporary coach bogies while No.1 (with exterior steps fitted and unfolded) illustrates the car with its power unit installed; note the solid upper panels on the end of No.3 and the very neat visual lines resulting from the use of inside cylinders and motion. (LMS Official — 2)

The LNWR cars were especially well built and were technically interesting by way of employing an *inside*-cylindered power unit. This certainly made them less grotesque when seen in motion from the outside and almost certainly made them more comfortable in ride quality if only because the cylinders were nearer to the carriage centre line. They also lasted better than most and even the ruthless LMS style of management found use for them until the late 1920s/early 1930s. One lasted (just) until BR days and when it was withdrawn from the Moffat branch of the old Caledonian Railway in 1948, it had become the final survivor of any of its kind in Great Britain.

The other rigid railcars came from the Midland and were not the best of their kind either in technicalities or appearance.

Their outside styling was vaguely reminiscent of the Midland's turn of the century square panelled stock, but without the famous clerestory and the first power units were unreliable and had to be changed. The interiors displayed unpleasant pierced plywood seating whose comfort is best left to the imagination. However, one was converted into an officers' saloon and as such, rescued by the NRM. Unfortunately, it has not, as yet, been possible to re-create its original state (it would be wickedly expensive one imagines, even as a non-working cosmetic project); but it is the only vehicle in Britain which could be restored to original form and it would be nice to see a working railcar again — a deserving case for National Lottery funding perhaps?

The second trio (Nos.4-6) of LNWR railcars, built in 1906, had some slight changes to the window arrangement on either side of the central passenger doors which can be appreciated by comparing the previous pictures with this view of No.4 at Bletchley early in its life (on Bedford branch duty). Soon after building, the LNWR cars had 5500 added to their numbers and this one became LNWR No.5504. Renumbered 10697 by the LMS after grouping, it was the only survivor beyond 1930 and became LMS No.29988 in 1933 — see next picture. (Pendragon Collection)

The first six LNWR steam railcars were by no means a failure. Though never as numerous as those of the GWR, they lasted roughly as long, none being withdrawn before 1927 and all having a better than 20 year working life. Five were withdrawn between 1927 and 1930 but the last survivor worked in traffic for over 40 years (probably something of a record) and is seen here at Moffat on 13th September 1939 as LMS No.29988. It was to work the ex-Caledonian Moffat branch from Beattock until 1948 and became the last British steam railcar of any type to be scrapped. (T. J. Edgington Collection)

The final LNWR steam railcar design was a one-off car, built in 1910 along with a purpose-built matching driving trailer No.1777. The ensemble is seen here at Lees, near Oldham, on 6th July 1910. Another attractive looking car, it was LNWR No.5507 from new, becoming LMS No.10700 after grouping and scrapped in 1928. The trailer fared rather better, though itself also a one-off. Built to run with No.5507, it became LMS No.5197 after grouping and No.15851 in 1933. It remained in use as a driving trailer for push-pull work until 1956. (LMS Official)

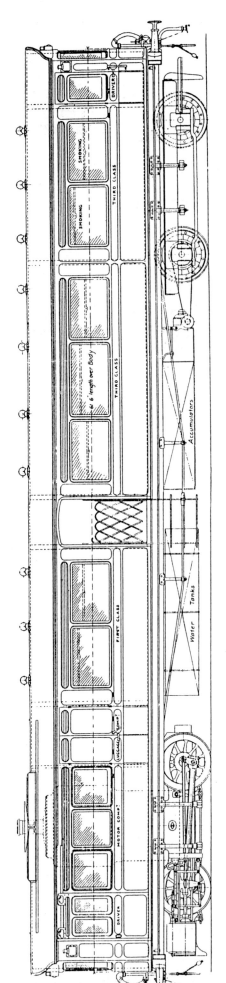

The Furness Railway built a highly attractive pair of steam railcars with equally good looking four-wheel trailers in 1905. The clerestory form (for the passenger areas only) was distinctly unusual for a steam railcar, but the aesthetic appeal of the ensemble can readily be appreciated from these two Edwardian vintage views of the opposite sides of No.1 and its trailer, taken at the Lakeside terminus of the branch from Ulverston. The cars were built at Barrow but only survived until c.1914. (Pendragon Collection — 2)

The three Great Central railcars of 1904-5 were stylish units which bore a striking similarity to the LNWR cars and also carried a slight hint of the contemporary locomotive hauled stock of the GCR in their visual lines. This is No.1, almost brand new judging from the state of the paintwork, at Barton station c.1905 and presumably working the Barton-New Holland service. (R. C. Riley Collection)

Initial impressions of the drawing of the GCR railcar may suggest that the window arrangement of the motor compartment windows does not comply with the photograph. What is not immediately apparent on the drawing is that the drivers door slides to open it and it is covering part of the motor compartment in the photograph. It will be noted though that the luggage compartment double doors were provided with droplights and not as shown on the drawing. Modellers should also note that the waist panel lettering on the drawing is for specification only and not as applied to the actual vehicle where the company title was shown at either end of the body. One final note to modellers is the eaves panel vent over the motor compartment which was flush with the side to enable clearance for the sliding door. In the brown and french gey livery of the period, the three railcars made a handsome sight. Scale: 4mm = 1ft

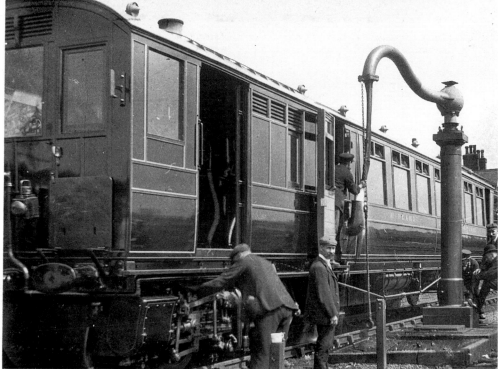

The somewhat less than satisfactory Midland steam railcars of 1904 were put in use between Morecambe and Heysham. This early view shows No.2234 taking water at Hellifield and given the ex-works appearance of the paint work, it is conceivable that the picture was taken when the car was new and en-route to its area of operation. (NRM Collection)

MR railcar No.2234 survives in 'saloon' form at the National Railway Museum — albeit in somewhat dilapidated state pending a restoration decision. This view, taken at Lichfield (Trent Valley) on 22nd August 1956, shows it in happier days on an Officers' special working as No.M45010M and painted in BR red/cream. Comparison with the previous view will show that apart from new windows at the former powered end, the carriage 'architecture' was very little changed. (F. W. Shuttleworth)

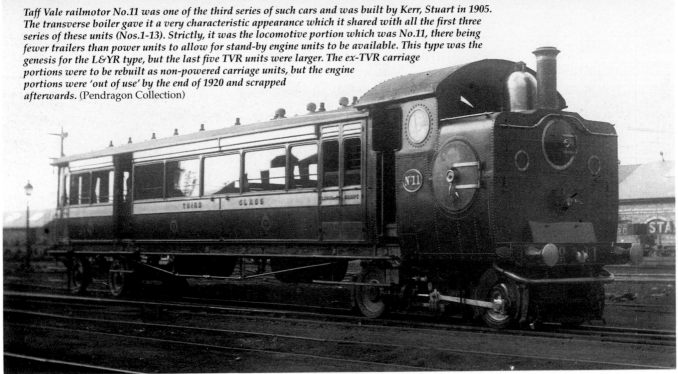

Taff Vale railmotor No.11 was one of the third series of such cars and was built by Kerr, Stuart in 1905. The transverse boiler gave it a very characteristic appearance which it shared with all the first three series of these units (Nos.1-13). Strictly, it was the locomotive portion which was No.11, there being fewer trailers than power units to allow for stand-by engine units to be available. This type was the genesis for the L&YR type, but the last five TVR units were larger. The ex-TVR carriage portions were to be rebuilt as non-powered carriage units, but the engine portions were 'out of use' by the end of 1920 and scrapped afterwards. (Pendragon Collection)

This view also shows TVR No.11, but from the opposite side, and gives a clearer impression of the carriage portion whose number was carried on the solebar and is hidden behind the guard! The original view just shows the obscured figure to be a '4' and since No.14 was one of the final series of longer carriages (the carriage portions were numbered in order of building), identification can be established as No.4, one of seven composite units, the other nine being all third. In 1921, along with five others (Nos.1, 5, 7, 8 and 12), it was altered to form a six-coach corridor train, becoming GWR composite No.6399, later all first No.8090. In original form, the Taff Vale cars were distributed widely on the parent system and this (undated) view shows the car on Pontypridd and Old Ynysybwl service — the destination board on the side reads simply 'Ynysybwl'. (R. C. Riley Collection)

The final Taff Vale railmotors (Nos.14-18) were altogether larger than the first three series with a double-ended cab casing and a longer passenger portion. This is No.14, clearly on the occasion of its delivery to the Taff Vale in 1906 from Brush Electrical, who fitted the bodies to the Manning Wardle engine units. (NRM Collection)

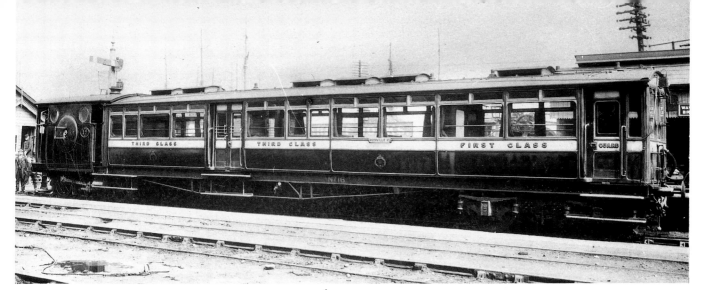

This view shows Taff Vale engine unit No.17 of the final series with the last of the carriage portions to be built, No.16. The location is probably Cardiff Bute Street — the destination board reads 'Woodville Rd', a location on the line from Bute Street to Maindy North Road Platform, one of the many routes on which the TVR cars operated. The carriage was converted in 1922 (along with Nos.6, 14 and 15) to form part of a four coach corridor train, becoming GWR 4025 in the process — see next view. (R. C. Riley Collection)

The articulated steam railcar

The articulated railcar was to fare little better than its rigid equivalent and in this category, we are dealing with an idea which was very much a brainchild of the Lancashire and York-shire Railway via the Taff Vale, for which latter railway Mr Hurry Riches had designed the first example in 1903. Mr Rich-es felt that a more powerful power unit, articulated to the pas-senger carrying portion, might be a better solution to the problem and delivered a technical paper on the subject to the I.Mech.E in 1906. His TVR examples had an unusual transverse boiler with single axle drive and the LYR decided to obtain two similar machines to the same basic design in 1905. They came from Kerr Stuart, but the LYR Chief Engineer, George Hughes, was not too enchanted with them and reckoned he could do better.

The Taff Vale cars were built between 1903 and 1905 in the form of one prototype and three main batches. There were 18 engine units and 16 carriage portions, thus permitting stand-by power units to be available — a practical idea which the LYR also copied. The pioneer power unit came from the company's own workshops (the last 'locomotive' to be built by the TVR in its shops at West Yard, Cardiff), followed by six each from Avonside and Kerr-Stuart and a final five from Manning War-dle, the last type being much more powerful than the first three series which were broadly identical. With the last units, the transverse boiler was retained but the bodywork also displayed a closed-in cab both behind and ahead of the boiler with the chimney position now to the rear.

The carriage portion of the TVR railcars was to Hurry Rich-es' own design and all were much the same save for the last

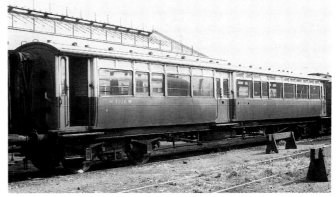

The carriage styling of the Taff Vale railmotors could be seen for many years, thanks to their rebuilding as 'ordinary' stock — see text. This view shows what had been Taff Vale railmotor car No.15, one of three built by Brush Electrical in 1906, mainly for use with the final series of more powerful engine units. In 1922, along with its two similar companions, it was converted to corridor third as seen here. As W4024W, it still carried the post war GWR livery (evidenced by the double waist lining) when seen at Caerphilly Works on 11th May 1954. (T. J. Edgington Collection)

three (built by Brush Electrical for the more powerful locomo-tive units). These displayed some differences, not least their considerably increased length.

As with most rigid railcars, the articulated Taff Vale units did not enjoy a long life in their original form. Half of the coach portions were converted to trailers and the other half to corri-dor carriages between 1914 and 1922 and the engine portions were all scrapped before the grouping. It is not quite clear to the writer why they did not last longer, given the size of the 'fleet' — almost identical to that of the LYR. Perhaps it was the usual problem of inadequate haulage power if patronage grew. Cer-tainly there is evidence that the transverse boilered engine was not unduly powerful and would certainly have had trouble with a trailer. And this was undoubtedly the reason why, hav-ing evaluated the Kerr Stuart units (above), the LYR designed its own version.

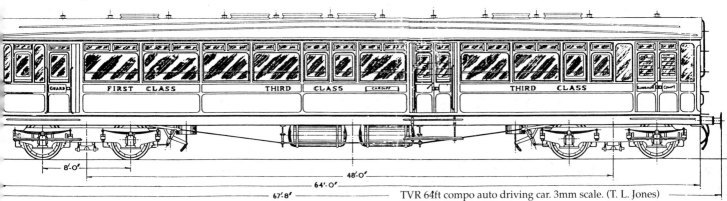

TVR 64ft compo auto driving car. 3mm scale. (T. L. Jones)

The influence of the Taff Vale design is very clear on this view of the first trial of Lancashire and Yorkshire unit No.2 at Burnley, the roof board being inscribed: 'Burnley (Bank Top), Nelson and Colne'. Built by Kerr, Stuart in 1905, the engine portion is an exact repeat of the Hurry Riches TVR type, but the LYR-designed carriage portion is rather more substantial. When Hughes decided to build his own railcars after only two Kerr Stuart units had been evaluated, the earlier carriage portions were retained to run with new locomotive portions, built in 1909 and taking the numbers of the Kerr Stuart engines which were then scrapped. (B. C. Lane Collection)

This view of Kerr Stuart LYR railmotor No.2 was taken c.1905-7 and shows the unit in service prior to the LYR design being built. The style of the carriage part is very well shown and the headboard reveals that it is on the Southport-Barton-Altcar & Hillhouse service, one of several trial workings introduced especially for the railmotors. (B. C. Lane Collection)

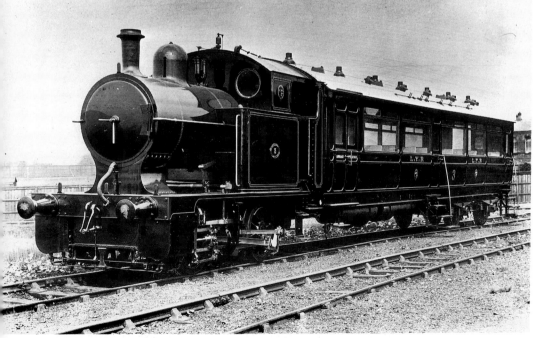

This fine official view shows the first Hughes design of LYR railmotor, No.3, when new in 1906. The engine part carries No.3 because the two Kerr Stuart engines carried Nos.1/2 and the LYR design continued the sequence. It was also the next to last withdrawal, being scrapped in mid-1947 as LMS No.10600. Note that the carriage has the same number as the engine (the figure 3 is not for third class!), the carriage parts of the Kerr Stuart units carrying Nos.1/2. (LMS Official)

At first, the carriage parts of the LYR railmotors had fully glazed ends, a feature well shown in this pre-1914 view at Stainland. It is tempting to assume that because the carriage part is No.3 that the engine element was also No.3. However (see text), there were eventually eighteen engines and only seventeen carriages, including the two non-standard original types, so the chances of a coincidence of numbers became ever more unlikely as time went by. In this case, the engine cannot be identified. (B. C. Lane Collection)

The result was the well known LYR design: a typically neat locomotive unit paired with an altogether better looking passenger 'carriage'. In this form, they became (marginally) the most numerous and undeniably the best articulated steam railmotors in Britain — and also by far the longest lived. For one thing, Hughes had designed a powerful enough engine to allow a trailer to be attached and this gave added flexibility at times of busier traffic. Standard boiler flange plates were incorporated, incidentally giving the same boiler diameter as the highly successful Aspinall 'A' Class 0-6-0. For the first time on the LYR (1906) Walschaerts valve gear was adopted and the driving wheels were coupled. They came into service between 1906 and 1911, matching trailer cars being provided from the beginning.

Although the two 'Taff Vale' type locomotive units were soon consigned to oblivion, to be replaced by the L&Y type, their carriage parts were retained and went into the total 'pool' and, along with the rest, survived to the LMS. Like the Taff Vale, the L&Y had gone for more locomotive than carriage units (18 and 17 respectively, the latter including the original pair). Leisurely withdrawal began in 1927 but the last survivor just managed to reach BR in 1948.

continued on page 26

In 1909, the LYR replaced the two Kerr Stuart engines with its own type of locomotive and their running numbers were re-used on the new units. They were in fact not built until Nos.3-15 of the Hughes type had appeared. In this view on the Rishworth branch, the new unit No.1 is paired, coincidentally, with carriage unit No.1 which had been built for the original Kerr Stuart engine, but such tidiness was not to last! (B. C. Lane Collection)

The new Hughes engine units were sufficiently powerful to justify the LYR designing a separate bogie trailer to run with the railmotors when traffic warranted such a move and these too were introduced in 1906, just after the first carriage portions had been built. In consequence, the original glazed ends of the carriages built by that time (Nos.1-8, including the first non-standard pair) were later modified to carry gangway connections. This view shows No.1 of the original two 1905 carriages thus modified, running with engine unit No.1, on the same occasion as the previous picture. For the record, carriages Nos.9-17 (all to the standard LYR design) were built new with gangwayed ends. (B. C. Lane Collection)

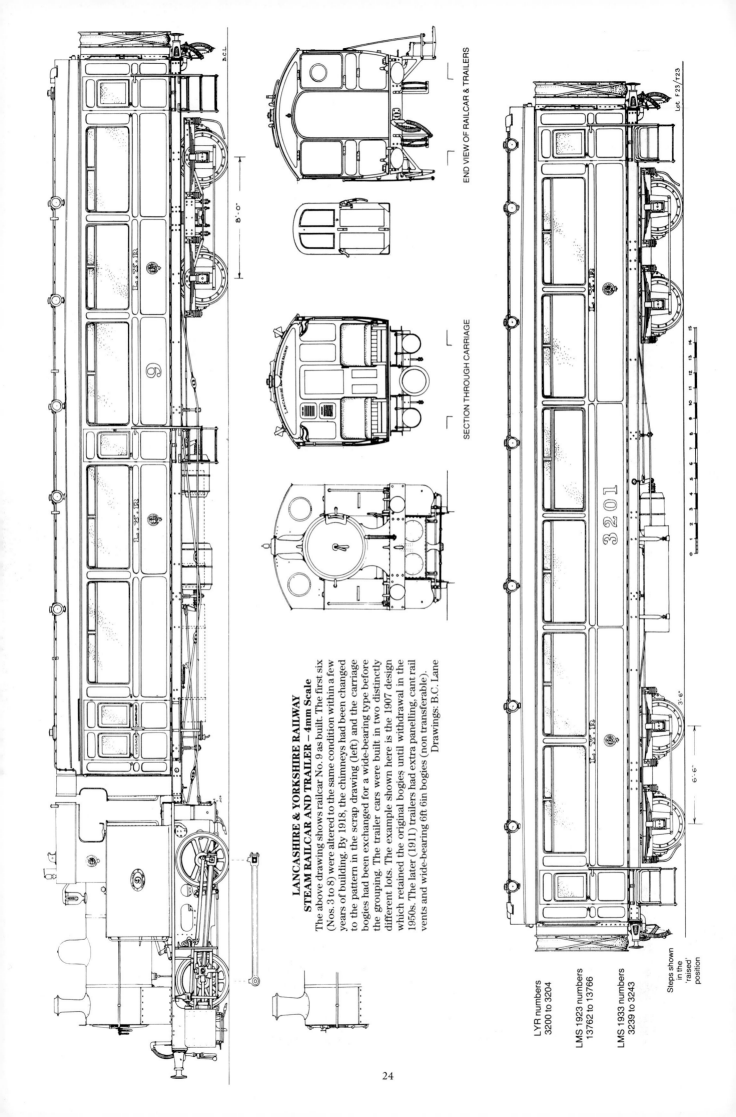

END VIEW OF RAILCAR & TRAILERS

SECTION THROUGH CARRIAGE

**LANCASHIRE & YORKSHIRE RAILWAY
STEAM RAILCAR AND TRAILER – 4mm Scale**

The above drawing shows railcar No. 9 as built. The first six (Nos. 3 to 8) were altered to the same condition within a few years of building. By 1918, the chimneys had been changed to the pattern in the scrap drawing (left) and the carriage bogies had been exchanged for a wide-bearing type before the grouping. The trailer cars were built in two distinctly different lots. The example shown here is the 1907 design which retained the original bogies until withdrawal in the 1950s. The later (1911) trailers had extra panelling, cant rail vents and wide-bearing 6ft 6in bogies (non transferable).

Drawings: B.C. Lane

LYR numbers
3200 to 3204

LMS 1923 numbers
13762 to 13766

LMS 1933 numbers
3239 to 3243

Steps shown
in the
'raised'
position

Lot. F 23/T23

Almost brand new LYR railmotor No.15, complete with its matching numbered carriage portion, is seen here on a Blackpool Fleetwood service at Poulton Curve Halt, c.1911, accompanied by one of the new purpose built trailer cars (unidentified).
(B. C. Lane Collection)

The LMS renumbered the LYR railmotors in two distinct series. The engine parts were numbered in the locomotive number series standardised in 1923 and became Nos.10600-17 in order of building at the head of the former LYR 'Passenger tank engine' block (which actually included all the smaller Cumbrian railways as well) while the carriage portions (and the purpose built trailer cars) were numbered in a quite separate LMS carriage series. Somewhat unusually, during the first LMS phase, the carriage numbers were carried in large numerals below the waist. Both these changes are seen in this c.1930 picture at Wakefield, showing No.10616 (ex-LYR No.17) along with carriage portion No.14692 (Ex-LYR No.10, second LMS No.29993), both elements being painted in the fully lined LMS crimson lake livery at the time. (T. J. Edgington Collection)

A later LMS condition is represented by this close-up view of No.10617 (ex-LYR No.18) at Bolton on 29th May 1938. The engine part is now black (with red lining), while the carriage portion carries the simple LMS post-1933 crimson livery with simplified horizontal lining. (NRM collection)

No.10617 (Ex-LYR No.18) was the last survivor, being withdrawn, without further renumbering, just three months into the BR period in 1948. This fine detail view, taken at Blackrod on 22nd April 1947 and clearly showing the gangwayed end, shows it in final state, attached to carriage portion No.29999, co-incidentally also the last carriage to be built: Ex-LYR No.17, 1st LMS No.14699. The number is now applied in normal carriage insignia on a plain red livery without lining. Note that some of the waist beading has vanished (replaced by new sheet steel panels after a repair) and that the windows still retain the partially blacked-out paint of the wartime years. (The late H. C. Casserley).

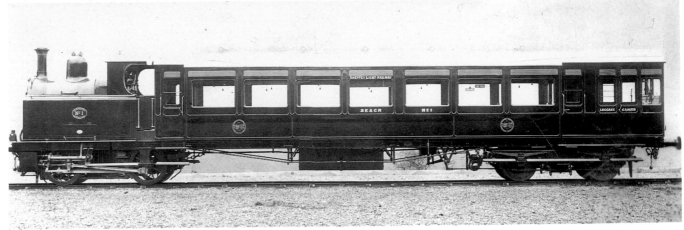

This side view of SE&CR railcar No.1, also inscribed for the Sheppey Light Railway, shows off the stylish lines of the carriage portion very well. After a few years on the Isle of Sheppey, No.1 went to Tonbridge for the Otford-Sevenoaks service in 1907, to Dover in 1910 for the Sandgate route and by 1914 was at Bricklayers Arms to work the Woodside to Selsdon Road service. It was 'set aside' in 1915. (NRM Collection)

Although numerically less significant than the rigid type, the articulated option was to sprout just as many variations and attracted the attention of a number of eminent locomotive engineers — perhaps because they looked more like 'real' trains? Be that as it may, most of them, however short-lived or unsuitable they may have been, were of more than usually pleasant visual aspect and a number are worth singling out for brief consideration.

The leading company after the TVR and LYR was, perhaps surprisingly, the South Eastern and Chatham Railway, for which concern its well known engineer, Harry Wainwright, supervised the design of eight beautifully stylish examples in 1904-5. All eight locomotive units were built by Kitsons and represented the first use of Belpaire boilers on the SE&CR. They were also unusual in being painted in carriage lake livery to match the carriage portion itself which followed standard SE&CR styling.

The first two differed slightly from the final six and like many others, they were found work for less time than had, no doubt, originally been hoped. More successful than many, and improved by some modifications over the years to improve

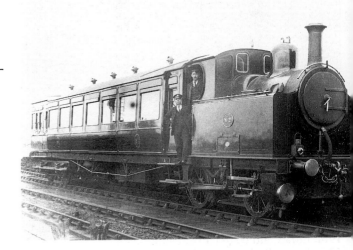

The SE&CR built eight railcars of which the first two (represented here by No.2) had rather longer side tanks than the final six, the deficiency being made good by well tanks. The two pioneer railcars were originally built for the Sheppey Light Railway (No.1 was actually inscribed as such), No.2 going to Hastings in 1907 for the Rye service, on which it spent most of its subsequent working life (save for a spell at Bricklayers Arms in 1910-11). It became one of the last two to survive, being laid aside in February 1920 along with No.7 of the second series. (Pendragon Collection)

The main batch of SE&CR cars is represented by this charming study of No.4 at Woodside, probably in late 1906 during one of several periods when the Selsdon Road to Woodside service was worked by the SE&CR rather than the LB&SCR. During its later life, No.4 was located at Orpington (Beckenham Junction-Crystal Palace service) and later at Slades Green for the Dartford-Gravesend service on which it seems to have spent much of its time apart from the odd trip on the Hundred of Hoo branch. No.4 was one of four cars kept in use after 1914 — see text — and was not officially 'laid aside' until June 1918, having latterly served the War Department light railway from Slades Green to the ammunition factory at Crayford Ness until the increased number of passengers began to outstrip the railcars' capacity early in 1918. (R. C. Riley Collection)

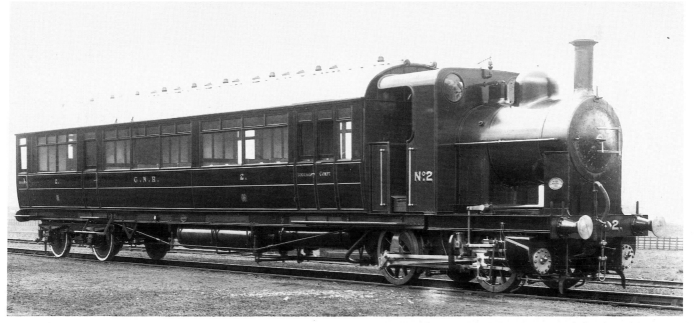

GNR railcar No.2 of the first pair. This works view, taken when the unit was new in 1905, clearly shows the high roof style adopted for the first time on these units. As can be seen, the locomotive portion (GNR built) was not too dissimilar to the Kitson design shown in a later view. In 1930, the passenger ends were converted to an articulated twin (Nos.44151-2) but only lasted until 1937 because of damage received in a mishap at Hatfield. (NRM Collection)

their efficiency, the railcars were, nevertheless, none too popular and all were ordered to be withdrawn before the end of 1914. In fact, although all were officially 'laid aside' between 1914 and 1920, the changed circumstances of the first World War caused half of them to remain in use as designed until 1918 and two lasted until 1920. Though officially 'out of use' after that time, all came to the Southern Railway in 1923 and in 1924, although the engine parts were condemned, the carriage portions were converted for auto-train work, in which role they were found useful for many a long year.

Ivatt too, on the Great Northern, became interested and had six units built (in three pairs) for evaluation — all differing

Interior view of GNR steam railcar No.2 looking towards the rear end of the unit. The seats were of throw-over type save where adjacent to the partitions and, as seen, could be arranged in mixed configuration if so required. (NRM Collection)

The three pairs of GNR steam railcars, though all built by different firms, shared a common carriage layout; but the last two pairs saw reversion to the older low roof carriage profile. No.6 was the second of two examples built by Kitson and Co. in 1905 (bodies by Birmingham C&W) and the engine part, though not too unlike the 'native' GNR product of the first two cars, especially in the shape of cab roof, also had features in common with the same firm's contemporary design for the SE&CR — eg the Belpaire boiler. Withdrawn in 1927 as railcars, the engines were scrapped; but the carriage parts were united into an articulated twin (Nos.44161-2) and lasted until February 1959, having served on the Horncastle Branch in its last days. (T. J. Edgington Collection)

slightly in detail though with internal carriage layout much the same in all cases. They were procured as part of a GNR experiment with self propelled passenger units and numbered in a new series as 1&2, 5&6, 7&8, the missing 3&4 being kept for two proposed petrol engined cars of which, in the event, only one was bought — see next Chapter.

The steam railcars were, perhaps, most famous in retrospect for the fact that the first pair had full height elliptical roofs, the first such time this profile had appeared on the GNR — clearly a reflection of the growing influence of Nigel Gresley, at that time Carriage and Wagon Chief to the GNR. However, and presumably as part of the experiment, all three pairs came from different firms and this seems likely to be the reason why the carriage portions of the last four reverted to the more traditional low roof GNR profile — presumably the GNR was not yet ready to standardise the new roof shape.

Though the cars lasted for quite a long time compared with many others, they were never intensively used and available sources suggest that only a few routes were regularly served by them: Louth-Grimsby; Hitchin-Baldock; Finchley-Edgware and the Chickenly Heath branch. By 1917, all six were out of use and their use over the next few years (if any) is unclear. Taken over by the LNER in 1923, it soon became clear that there was no further use for them in original mode. Hardly surprisingly, and presumably influenced by Nigel Gresley's support for the idea as a weight saving device, the carriage parts were converted into articulated 'twins' between 1925 and 1930 and the engine portions withdrawn.

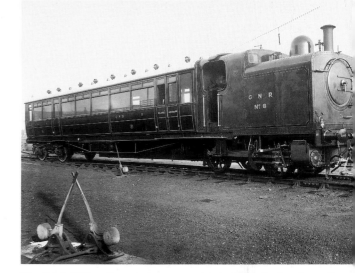

The third GNR railcar design, appearing in 1906, displayed a rather brutish looking engine portion built by Avonside (carriage bodies from Bristol C&W) and, in the event, turned out to be, marginally, the shortest lived of the three types. No.8 is shown here, revealing an engine casing which cloaked most of the fitments. This did not last long and was removed in 1907 to reveal a somewhat ungainly looking locomotive compared with the altogether more purposeful outline of that used on the first four railcars, though with much the same power. As with all GNR railmotors, water tanks were to be found below the carriage portion. (NRM Collection)

This excellent official view was taken at Doncaster in September 1925 when the carriages from GNR railcars Nos.7/8 had been converted to articulated twin Nos.44141/2. As can be seen, this involved a slight lengthening at the outer ends of the original carriages, but the major portion, with its large windows, remained much as before. The unit shown was condemned in August 1958 and worked the Essendine-Bourne branch until 1951 and afterwards in such widespread locations as Mablethorpe, Newcastle-Hawick and finally, Bridlington-Scarborough. The low roof conversion of railcars 5/6 was to the same design as shown here. (LNER Official)

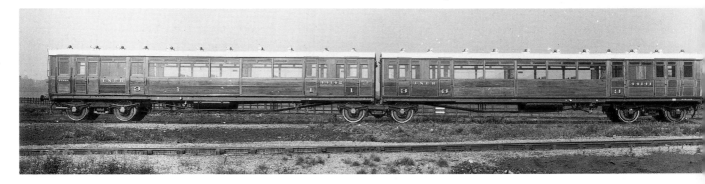

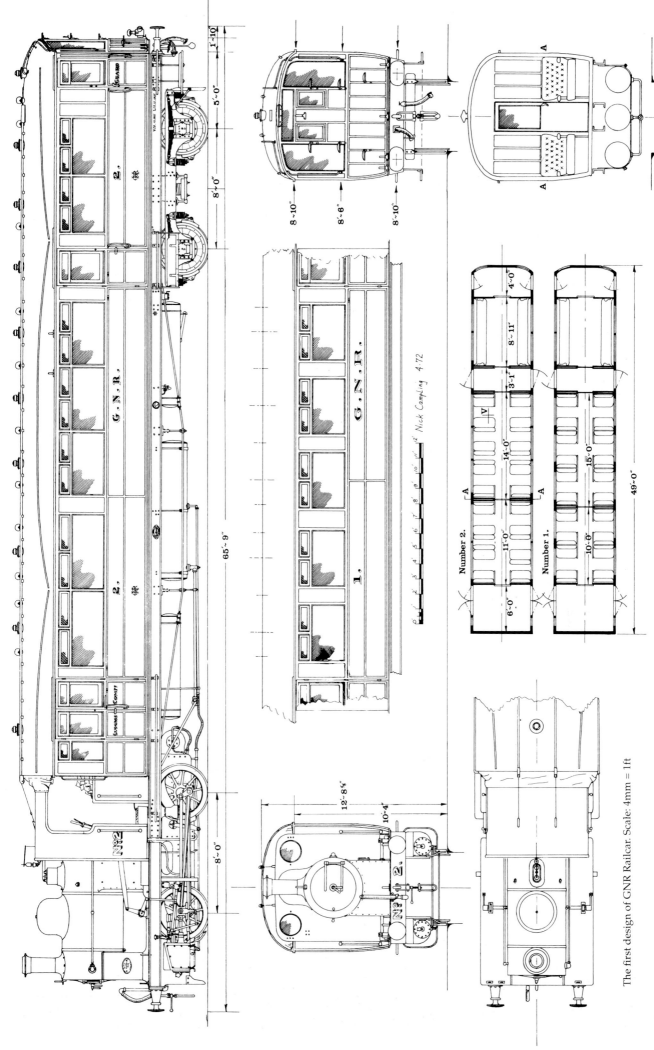

The first design of GNR Railcar. Scale: 4mm = 1ft

This superb view shows LB&SCR railcar No.1 when brand new in 1905. As with many railcars, the carriage bodywork (built by the Electric Railway and Tramway Carriage Works) did not mirror normal company stock of the day but was very stylish. The car was officially withdrawn in 1919 and sold to the Trinidad Government Railways in November of that year. (SR Official).

Of the rest of this group, the LB&SCR and North Staffordshire examples had much in common, both being built by Beyer-Peacock in 1905-6. They displayed a sort of cross-bred powered end, partially enclosed but with smokebox front and chimney projecting in a rather quaint fashion beyond the 'cab' — probably very practical for cleaning purposes. The engine portions were identical on both railways but the carriage portions displayed different styling — those of the Brighton line being rather neater. Fortunately, as is often the way with these things, both types were reasonably well recorded photographically, especially those of the NSR, and a fair selection of views can be offered.

That said, however, the LB&SCR examples did not seem to be well received and only lasted for a few years, albeit not withdrawn for some time. The NSR examples, by contrast, ran until 1922. They were curious and rather ungainly looking things (by comparison with most in this group) with a sort of tramcar-like passenger part, but they must have generated a bit of revenue during the 16 years or so before they went the way of the rest.

At this point and again talking of appearances, mention should be made of the only GWR excursion into this type — a pair of Kerr Stuart cars with hideous enclosed cabs and non-GWR carriage styling. They were, presumably, withdrawn by the GWR because of their non-standard configuration compared with those in the main fleet. One of them was sold to the Nidd Valley Light Railway in 1920 and named *Hill*. It managed to outlive all the GWR steam railcars of any kind, being withdrawn in 1937. It was still in existence in a Leeds scrapyard in 1962!

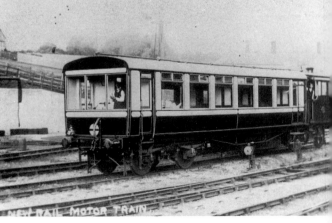

These c.1905 views of LB&SC railcar No.2 allow appreciation to be made of the slightly different body arrangement compared with No.1: note the rather shorter 'luggage' portion with what was otherwise identical styling. It was photographed at St Leonards Marina and one of the views (a contemporary postcard) states 'New rail Motor train' which indicates that it was first used on some form of south coast shuttle in the direction of Eastbourne. The writer is unable to offer further information about the use made of either this or the other LB&SCR car. (Pendragon Collection — 2)

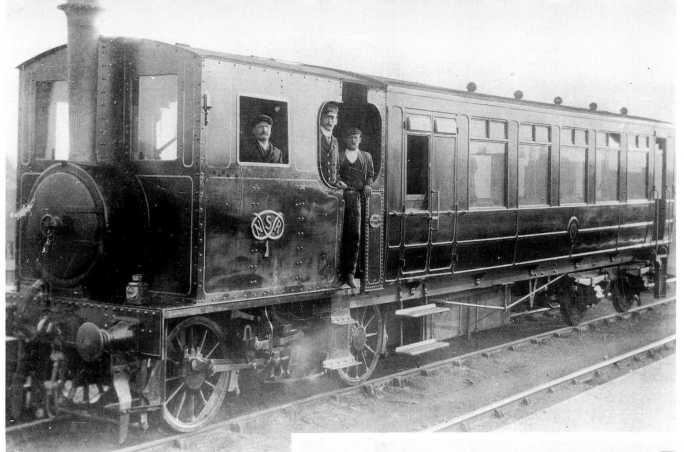

These opposite side views of North Staffordshire railcar No.1 indicate the strong visual locomotive similarities to the Brighton cars, but also show the somewhat less stylish bodywork. The left hand side view (with the crew proudly posing — the car was probably quite new!) shows the original form of raised metal NSR 'Knot' and number while the right hand side picture displays the later insignia style. Neither picture can be dated, nor are the locations known. (Pendragon Collection — 2)

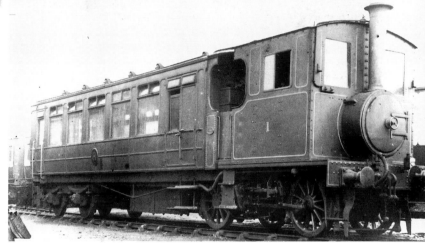

NSR railcar No.2 was identical to No.1 and this attractive view shows it in service at Oakamoor when still obviously very new — other details of the service not specified. From this angle of view, the rather 'box-shaped' appearance is less apparent and the unit makes an attractive picture in the typical rural surroundings for which many railcars were originally intended. (T. J. Edgington Collection)

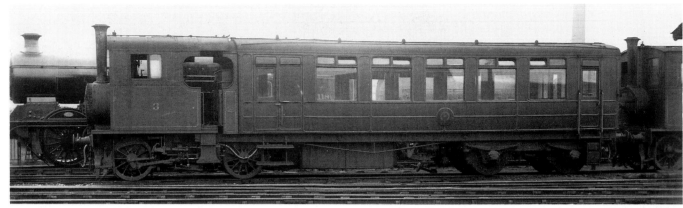

Other than the TVR, many other independent small Welsh railways introduced steam railcars in penny numbers — again see Table I. Of the so far unmentioned systems, two chose the articulated type, both of more than passing interest. The Rhymney Railway pair of 1907 were yet another product of the imaginative Hurry Riches (who had now moved from the TVR) and he seems to have learned a lesson from George Hughes, for the engine portions were much bigger than those of the TVR and had their boilers conventionally disposed. They were also designed to pull an extra six-wheel coach if needed. Even so, they lasted a very short time, the carriages (of a stylish 'modern' looking type) being converted to normal coaching stock in 1910 and 1919 while the engines enjoyed a new lease of life when altered to 0-6-0T form.

The solitary Port Talbot Railway car of 1906 was interesting in a number of ways. Firstly, it was the only articulated British steam railcar of the pre-World War I period to have a properly integrated 'carriage style' locomotive portion. Secondly, it was the only British railcar of any kind to have a six-coupled engine portion and lastly, it was the only GWR 'constituent company' railcar to survive in its original form. The GWR (which acquired the PTR in 1908) never converted it into an auto-trailer, though its panelled styling was not dissimilar to that of the 'home grown' product, and it was sold, intact, to the Port of London Authority in 1920, along with two other 'proper' GWR railcars and continued in service until 1926.

NSR railcar No.3 was also built in 1905 but appeared in December, some six or seven months after the first two. Although the general arrangement does not seem to have changed in any significant way, the higher more rounded roof on both locomotive and carriage portions gives a more harmonious look to the ensemble compared with the earlier pair, of which the locomotive end of one example can just be seen on the right. This is a later period view (the Class F 0-6-4T in the background dates only from 1916) but the location is not specified. However, a reliable source states that the cars were used for local services in the Stoke-on-Trent area and the presence of the tank engine suggests a more substantial sized location — possibly even Stoke itself. (Pendragon Collection)

Ex-GWR railcar No.15 was one of a pair of Kerr Stuart units (built in 1905 to the maker's design with bodies from Bristol Wagon and Carriage Company) which were quite unlike any of the 'home built' GWR railcars. In 1920 it was sold as a complete unit to J. F. Wake being re-sold to the Nidd Valley Light Railway in 1921 and named Hill. The NVLR was owned by Bradford Corporation Waterworks and operated in connection with the building of new reservoirs at the head of Nidderdale. The full title can be seen in the carriage waist panel and the Bradford 'arms' (as applied to municipal transport) appears on the lower panels. The picture was taken alongside the signal box at Pateley Bridge (NVLR) where the light railway made connection with the NER branch from Harrogate via Ripley Junction. The power unit had a transverse boiler and the name (hardly visible on this view) was painted on the side of the engine at waist height below the boiler doors. The shutters in the upper part of the cab opening were a post-GWR modification. (B. C. Lane Collection)

Rhymney Railway Railcar No.1 at Bargoed c.1908-10. It not only reveals the much more powerful engine unit adopted by Hurry Riches after his Taff Vale cars, but also its stylish passenger portion and its trailer hauling capability (see text). No.1 was built in 1907 and ran in railcar configuration until 1919 when the locomotive part was converted for further use — see next view. (T. J. McCarthy from R. C. Riley Collection)

This fascinating view shows the post-railcar state of the engine portion of one of the two Rhymney Railway railcars — a rare example of the re-use of such a unit after the railcars themselves had been withdrawn. No.121 was built as a powerful 0-4-0T unit for railcar No.1 in 1907 and carried this number until rebuilt in 1919 to the form shown here. The rebuild had extended frames, a new and larger combined coal bunker/water tank (instead of the previous short side 'tank' ahead of the cab) and a third pair of coupled wheels. In spite of its purposeful air, it did not last very long; as GWR No.662, it was withdrawn in June 1925. (T. J. Edgington Collection)

The NVLR proper ran only to Lofthouse-in-Nidderdale from whence a complex network of further 'private' lines, but still under the control of Bradford Corporation, penetrated the upper reaches of the dale. This picture, taken at Lofthouse in the 1920s, was made the subject of a contemporary postcard from which this image is taken. It shows the character of the passenger portion of Hill very well and the unit is thought to have been painted in 'Metropolitan' dark red (a favourite livery of the BCWW); while its generally smart appearance suggests that it was either soon after acquisition from the GWR or not long after an overhaul. The NVLR closed to public passenger service at the end of 1929, thereafter being operated as a private railway not requiring parliamentary sanction. (R. C. Riley Collection)

The Isle of Wight Central Railway also had a lone railcar, a workmanlike unit which ran from 1906 until being sold out of service in 1918. Like all the best of its kind, it had a properly adequate locomotive portion and had its proposed partner ever materialised (the company could not afford it!), who knows what the outcome might have been? The unit was, apparently, highly regarded in its early days because of its operational economy.

Only two Scottish companies tackled the steam railcar and both favoured the articulated 'visible engine' variant and even then only five existed 'in toto'. The Glasgow and South Western trio were typically neat units (lasting until 1917), two to one design and a third slightly different; while the Great North of Scotland pair were of some slight technical interest in that they had patent boilers with hemispherical firebox. This did not save the GNSR cars from early withdrawal; both were ineffective and survived only a few years.

So it was that for the most part, the steam railmotor was born, matured and died within less than a single generation before the grouping, with only the GWR and LYR examples (plus the odd one or two elsewhere) giving any sort of reasonable return on investment. Be they rigid or articulated, they represented, for the most part, a fascinating if ultimately abortive attempt by the railways to make a significant change.

They usually failed because of their inflexibility, only remaining viable in the purely contradictory sense of not generating too much extra patronage. When any sort of overloading became a problem, most of them could not offer enough power to move an extra trailer. Not surprisingly, the moment the railways began to consider using larger power units,

The solitary Isle of Wight Central railcar No.1 was built in September 1906 by R. W. Hawthorn & Co. (engine) and Hurst, Nelson & Co. (carriage), from whose works at Motherwell it was worked in steam to Southampton Docks to save time and expense. Designed for and put to work on the Merstone to Ventnor Town service, it was transferred to the Freshwater line in 1908. Although highly regarded in terms of economy by a railway always 'strapped for cash', it was, apparently, prone to oscillation and, to use a favourite phrase of the time, 'laid aside' in November 1910. The carriage re-appeared with an extra bogie and went into normal stock; while the engine, somewhat unusually for the genre, was given a small bunker and used at Newport for occasional shunting duty, before being sold in 1918. (Pendragon Collection)

thoughts turned to the more conventional locomotive plus train. This begat the altogether more successful auto-train (or Push-Pull unit, to use the common alternative expression) which many railways eventually adopted but which is outside the scope of this review.

But this did not stop the pursuit of self-propulsion so we must now turn to the next part of the story.

This view of G&SWR railcar No.1 leave one in no doubt that it was of more than pleasing appearance, the engine portion carrying the very neat Manson styling and the carriage being typical of contemporary 'Sou West' practice. The car was entirely 'home grown', so to speak, being built at Kilmarnock in 1904. The apparent side tanks housed 15cwt coal, water being carried in a 500 gallon well tank. No.2 was identical and the duties operated by them included the Catrine branch and from Ardrossan to Largs and Kilwinning. (T. J. Edgington Collection)

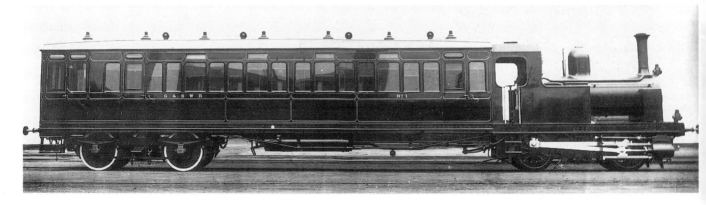

G&SWR railcar No.1, the first of its type in Scotland, was based at Ayr and first used on the Catrine branch shuttle to Mauchline where it was known as the 'Catrine Caur' (Car). This view is likely to have been taken on the inaugural run and although its reception by footplate staff was variable, the late David L.Smith states: "You could kindle her in the morning at Ayr with a barrowful of coal, dump another barrowful on the footplate, and away you went. 6am 'workers' to Annbank and then on to Mauchline to begin the day's shuttle service to Catrine." The Catrine branch was also the last line to see the railcars and when it was closed at the end of 1916, the railcars did no further work. (T. J. Edgington Collection)

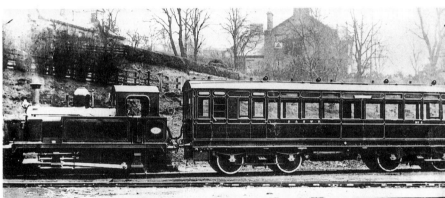

The two Great North of Scotland Railway steam railcars were also of more than averagely stylish appearance, made more distinctive by the use of a patent hemispherical boiler. This view shows No.29 (probably when quite new) at an unrecorded location. Dating from 1905, they did not have a long life; but the writer is unable to give a withdrawal date nor confirm the route(s) on which they might have worked. (NRM Collection)

G&SWR railmotor No.3 (built 1905) was slightly different from the first two, having a completely separated locomotive and carriage portion with conventional drawgear. Whether it is proper to include it here may be argued but it was designed as an integrated concept, believed originally intended for the Moniaive branch on which one of the G&SWR railmotors certainly ran. As ever, a neat 'Kilmarnock' solution was achieved, this time with a conventional coal bunker and side tanks on the locomotive. It will also be noted that the carriage portion, though stylistically very similar to Nos.1 and 2, had a more 'panoramic' arrangement of windows. All three G&SWR railmotors had the open saloon type of interior. (LMS Official)

The LB&SCR four-wheel railcars from Dick, Kerr and Co. drew on the latter company's electric tramcar experience, albeit powered by Petrol engines. Their running numbers (3/4) were clearly in sequence with the two steam railcars Nos.1/2 and were obviously part of a Brighton line evaluation of railcars of both types — see previous chapter. This is the first example, No.3, photographed when new, whose distinctive clerestory style body is of typically elaborate nature. (SR Official)

Chapter Three

ENTER INTERNAL COMBUSTION

DURING THE EARLY PART OF THIS CENTURY — and in the absence of sufficient traffic potential to go for full scale electrification — it was rather inevitable that the new fangled internal combustion engine would be tried out in some form or other as an alternative to steam and in Britain, this led to a minor outbreak of mildly comical petrol driven railcars. Some of these were direct drive but others were of petrol-electric configuration in which the engine generated electrical energy for traction motors, an idea pursued quite widely in North America and with some success; but the British contribution was minuscule.

The North Eastern Railway was the front runner and tried harder than most, more or less concurrently with its much more successful 'straight electrics' for the Tyneside area. Other modest offerings were chipped in by the GWR, GCR, GNR and, of all companies, the LB&SCR, the latter two companies making

use of some near-identical Kerr-Stuart four-wheelers displaying tramcar-like styling. They were neat machines but, like those of the NER, they came to nought; both types are illustrated but little is on record of either of them.

The internal combustion engine undoubtedly 'grew up' during the first World War, stimulated both on the land and in the air by the demands of the military. In consequence, many

---

The second Brighton petrol railcar, though mechanically much the same as No.3, had an altogether more 'modern' styling — but no reason has been discovered as to why the change took place; both cars were built at much the same time, 1904-5. The author has no record of the services operated, but they did not last for more than a few years. By 1911, they had been taken off passenger service and re-assigned as inspection cars for use on the new overhead electric lines.
(Tom Middlemass Collection)

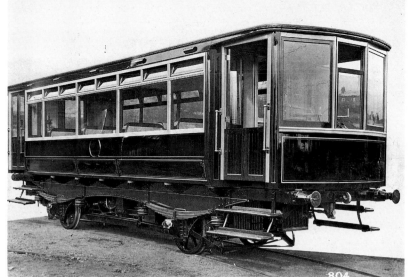

GNR No.3 was the solitary four-wheel petrol car which the company obtained from Dick Kerr, though a second was envisaged and No.4 allocated to it; but only one was taken into stock. The design had clear visual affinity with the second Brighton car but had rather larger end doors thus allowing the suppression of the centre door. It was at first given a two-colour livery (shades not specified) as shown here, but was later given the varnished wood livery as shown in the second view. It is also possible that all three body styles represented in this survey were determined by the makers themselves, who were anxious to have the cars tried out. Be that as it may, the GNR car was no more successful than the LB&SCR examples. It was tried in the Hatfield-Hertford area but without much success and by 1908 it had been withdrawn. (NRM Collection)

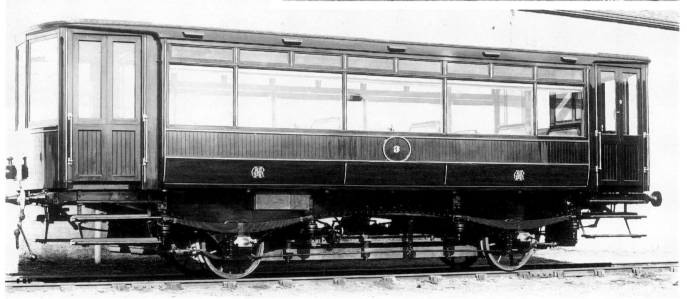

ex-servicemen resumed their civilian lives with more than an adequate working knowledge of this relatively new form of prime mover. Aided by a vast supply of government surplus ex-military omnibuses and lorries sold off at knockdown prices, thousands of former soldiers set up road transport businesses, both passenger and freight. The latter was, in the longer run, the more damaging to railway fortunes, but even in the former case, the rise of the motor bus in the 1920s and 1930s was a very real threat to railway passenger business, nowhere more than in the sort of services with which this survey is concerned.

At first, there were many who advocated a straight transfer of this new form of road technology to the rail, believing in all seriousness that all that was needed was to purchase a cheap lorry or bus engine, mount it on something approximating to a rail-borne equivalent of a road vehicle chassis, add some form of bodywork and off we go. They probably knew that a prime characteristic of rail transport meant that a given unit of power can shift between four and six times as large a load on smooth rails than on the rougher surfaced roads. It still can, of course and this realisation goes right back to the days when it was discovered that one horse could move the same sort of stage coach body mounted on railway wheels as it would take four or six to shift along the road. But in terms of mechanical power it was by no means as simple as that.

Essentially, the road vehicle power unit and transmission only reached its own when allied with pneumatic tyres to cushion the vibrations. Even the solid tyres of many older road vehicles gave some help in this regard; but the high frequency vibrations and rigid quality of most railway track were less forgiving and caused problems. Moreover, the lower power to weight ratio needed on the railways led to disappointing per-

formance and a tendency to overload, simply because it was in theory within the engine capacity to cope with such loads.

Thus, the first internal combustion railway vehicles prior to and during the immediate post-grouping era often seemed like fugitives from the highways, either with conventional road vehicle outline or a hint of tramcar practice in some of their styling. Though they did have some success, they were largely by way of individual experiments and few, if any, were multiplied beyond the first one or two units to be built. Some were distinctly quaint, viewed in retrospect, and for maybe ten years or so after the grouping, steam advocates probably saw no threat; in any case, were not the new steam railcars (Chapter 4) proving far more effective? This may have been so, up to a point, but some of the ideas introduced are still interesting to review in the context of later evolution.

As we have seen, the NER, an often under-rated concern, possibly because of its 'non-London' location, had long been a pioneer in 'alternative' solutions and right to the very end of its existence was still looking at both petrol-electric and direct drive solutions. Of all the pre-1923 companies, it does seem to have persevered rather more than most and its first efforts, a pair of petrol electric 'autocars', as it called them, emerged as early as 1903. They each had a single 85hp engine to drive a dynamo generating 550V for two 55hp motors.

Their styling was much influenced by the contemporary Tyneside electrics, complete with clerestory, and their neat outline was somewhat reminiscent of some of the 'enclosed' steam railmotors already considered. They were tried in a number of areas in their early years, including a summer stint between Filey and Scarborough during 1906-8, but they eventually came to rest in the Selby area during 1908, mostly for use on the Cawood branch, whence they remained for the rest of their

Petrol Electric autocar No.3171 was one of two vehicles built by the NER in 1903 and is seen here as first built in NER lake livery, though shortly afterwards it was repainted red and cream, possibly before going into service. In 1908 it went to the Selby area where it spent the rest of its existence being later joined by its partner No.3170. It seems that neither did much work after the grouping, most tasks usually being performed by the NER Leyland rail bus until 1926. No.3171 stood out of service for some years before being withdrawn in May 1930. (NRM Collection)

The interior of one of the two NER petrol electric autocars showing the rather heavy decor and throw-over tramcar type seating. Note the lavish provisioning for 'straphanging' standing passengers. (NRM Collection)

lives, save for a short stint by one of them in the Harrogate area during 1923. Although not withdrawn until 1930-31, they do not seem to have had much use after the mid-1920s; but at least they lasted a good deal longer than many a contemporary steam railmotor.

The next NER effort was a somewhat comical rail motor bus built in 1922 — in fact it was converted from a conventional road bus of Leyland manufacture a year or so earlier. It commenced work in the York area, operating to village stations within a few miles of the city and the appended picture gives a clear impression of its style. It was replaced by a petrol autocar (below) and sent off to Selby, where it seems to have had a busy life until destroyed in a fire in late 1926.

It was neither rebuilt nor replaced, but a similar idea found favour with the nearby Derwent Valley Light Railway, not to mention quite a few other lines of similar ilk. A contemporary drawing of the DVLR unit (appended) shows a back-to-back arrangement of twin bus units of Ford Duplex origin, but the writer is unable to offer further details save to say that in 1926 the pair of them were sold to the County Donegal Railways Joint Committee and regauged for use on that well known Irish 3ft gauge system .

A similar Ford-built back-to-back arrangement was also tried by the Kent and East Sussex in 1923 which was seemingly good enough to tempt the company to get another pair a year later, not to mention a single unit 'bus' from the Wolseley-Siddeley company. Meanwhile, the Shropshire and Montgomeryshire Railway went one better in 1923 with a triple unit — essentially another back-to-back set with an intermediate non-powered 'trailer' of matching style — and in 1928, the West Sussex Railway got into the act with yet another back-to-back unit, this time from the Shefflex Motor Company near Sheffield. In this context, we might also mention the impoverished Weston, Clevedon and Portishead Light Railway which twice tried to improve its disastrous finances by introducing internal combustion, a story told in more detail in *Bedside Backtrack* (Atlantic Transport Publishers 1993).

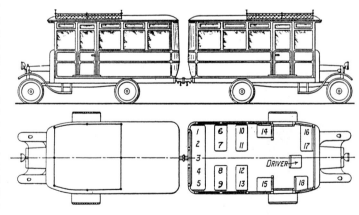

Elevation and plan of the Ford Duplex petrol-engined railcar. The principle was to use the leading car towing the other. The unit therefore could work in either direction without having to turn.

NER No.110 was described as a 'Petrol Rail Motor Bus', for once a fairly accurate description. Although three were apparently authorised, this was the only one to be acquired and its running number was taken from the NER road vehicle fleet series. It was soon renumbered 130 in the coach stock series and then became LNER No.130Y. After a short spell in the York area, it went to Selby in mid-1923 whence it remained save for an interesting diversion to Darlington in 1925 for the Stockton and Darlington Centenary. After the 1926 fire (see text), it was decided not to replace it and the unit was withdrawn in April 1927.
(LNER Official)

It is perhaps significant that most of these quaint innovations were at the behest of the formidable Col. H. F. Stephens, that memorable early 20th Century advocate of light railways who controlled many of the above-named systems. And indeed, if these road-derived vehicles were to be of any long-term significance, then the 'light railway' environment was obviously the best bet. But the main line companies for the most part seemed considerably less interested, though the NER was to persist for a little longer than most.

Following on the Leyland motor bus, and appearing just after the grouping, was a so-called 'Petrol Autocar', authorised by the NER in Autumn 1922. This looked rather like a short conventional carriage with a single powered axle at one end and a smaller-wheeled carrying bogie at the other. It appeared in mid-1923 and immediately replaced the above-mentioned

Leyland bus in the York area and was found much work to the surrounding villages until many station closures in 1930 left it with little to do. It went off to the Hull area for a few years but the introduction of Sentinel steam railcars seems to have severely curtailed its activities and it was withdrawn in 1934.

Although to NER design, 'Petrol Autocar' No.2105Y was not in fact built until LNER days and this view shows it ex-works in July 1923. Like the Leyland bus, it too took part in the S&D Centenary parade in 1925, while in August 1926 it was renumbered 22105. At 17.25T it was quite a substantial vehicle and perhaps the most conventional looking of the various NER experimental designs, bearing a close visual similarity to the company's locomotive hauled stock.
(LNER Official)

Petrol Inspection Car No.3711 was built by the NER in 1908, designed for use by officers inspecting the line. It had six extremely comfortable seats in the central saloon and was reputedly capable of reaching 55mph with a fuel consumption of 12mpg. Buffers were later provided and it was to spend most of its time at Darlington. In spite of the fact that the later cars of this group were newer and bigger, it was destined to have the longest life of the three, since all were withdrawn at the same time: February 1939.
(Pendragon Collection)

NER No.3768 was one of a pair built in 1912, drawing on the experience of No.3711 but some six feet longer and about twice the weight. These cars could seat twelve, but because of the extra side panelling, the all-round visibility was not quite as good. No.3768 was usually based at York and virtually destroyed in a fire at York South shed in 1921. Condemned in 1922, it was replaced late in 1923 by another car of similar but not quite identical style, carrying the same number — see next view.
(LNER Official)

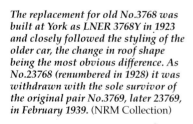

The replacement for old No.3768 was built at York as LNER 3768Y in 1923 and closely followed the styling of the older car, the change in roof shape being the most obvious difference. As No.23768 (renumbered in 1928) it was withdrawn with the sole survivor of the original pair No.3769, later 23769, in February 1939. (NRM Collection)

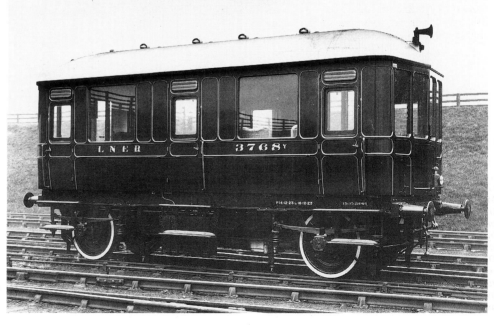

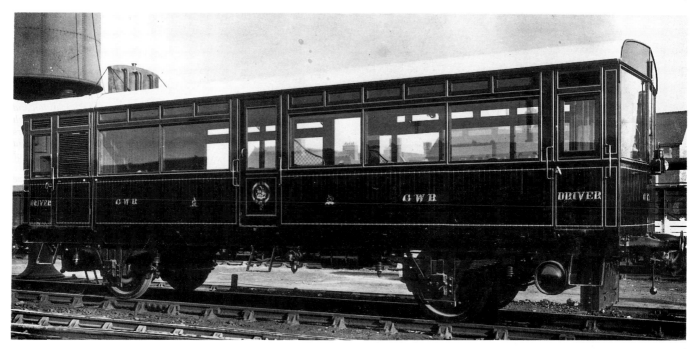

The solitary GWR petrol-electric car came from British Thompson Houston in 1911. Fitted with a 40hp Maudsley engine driving a dynamo connected to two motors and capable of 35mph, it was No.100 in the railmotor list and is seen here ex-works in the all lake livery which the GWR adopted for a period during the early 20th Century. (NRM Collection)

It is arguable whether the final NER internal combustion offering should appear in this survey at all, for the railcars concerned were not for revenue purposes. They were inspection cars but surely deserve mention if only because, collectively, they enjoyed more than thirty years of use — probably the longest working life of any pre-BR petrol or diesel driven railcars. In 1908, the NER introduced a small six-seat direct drive petrol car with four wheels and added two 'stretched' versions with some twice the power, weight and seating capacity (though only one third longer) in 1912.

All three displayed neat outlines in a traditionally NER panelled style and No.3768 of the 1912 pair is illustrated. This car was destroyed in a fire during 1921 but a replacement unit was immediately authorised. Taking the same number, it came out in 1923, a foot longer than the original 3768 with full elliptical roof, but otherwise very similar in style. Re-engined between 1929 and 1931, all three cars lasted until 1939. They were 40% cheaper to operate than the normal conventional saloon plus locomotive but appear to have been withdrawn largely because a locomotive could do other work as well as haul a saloon, whereas the railcars lay idle between duties. Even so, like the NER passenger carrying petrol cars, they could hardly be counted a failure.

All told, therefore, the overall NER experiment with internal combustion can be counted as a very near miss. Quaint they may have looked in some cases, but the company clearly obtained rather more value from them than had many railways with more conventional steam railcars.

At much the same time as the NER introduced its inspection cars, the GWR and GCR each assayed a petrol electric railcar (1911 and 1912 respectively). The GWR example came from the British Thomson-Houston Co., a slab-sided four-wheel car with matchboard panelling. Its overall appearance rather anticipated that of the Clayton LNER trailers, as did its active life (see Chapter 4). The GWR only kept it until 1919 (having latterly used it on the Windsor branch), after which it was sold to Lever Brothers where it enjoyed another four years semi-private use on the Port Sunlight system before withdrawal.

The GCR 'Bollington Bug', as it was later known, was a petrol-electric car and began its life by undertaking trials in both the Manchester and London areas. This view shows it at that time, working from Marylebone somewhere on the GCR/Metropolitan joint line — note the early Metropolitan clerestory multiple unit stock in the background; since the car was third class only, first class accommodation is provided by the middle compartments of the six-wheel trailer. In 1914 it returned north, first at Dinting and later at Macclesfield, where it remained until withdrawn in 1935. Built in 1912, it did not have a GCR running number but after the grouping, the LNER gave it the number 51907. (T. J. Edgington Collection)

This picture, taken from what is thought to have been an official coloured postcard, represents the only known view of the ex-LYR Manchester area electric unit housing a Beardmore 500hp diesel engine in 1927. It is not certain whether or not the unit was actually repainted in LMS colours but by that date, the real electric units were appearing in red, so this image may be correct.
(B. C. Lane Collection)

The GCR car of 1912 fared rather better. It was built by Westinghouse and bore more than a passing resemblance to the broadly contemporary 'tramcars' of the GCR's Grimsby and Immingham system. The seating too was of tramway type: rattan-covered with 'throw-over' backs. It was tried out in the Manchester and London areas, in the latter of which it often hauled a six-wheel trailer — see picture. Moving north again in 1914, it was first operated between Dinting and Glossop and after the First World War, settled down to fourteen years of hard use on the Macclesfield-Bollington shuttle service whereon it was known as the 'Bollington Bug'. Like some of the NER examples, it was eventually replaced by a Sentinel railcar.

At this point, mention should also be made of the Lancashire & Yorkshire Railway which had planned the application of petrol engines to lightweight railcars. In 1923 (under LMS auspices), diagrams were made to trial equivalent bus type vehicles on rails; the LYR already had a small fleet of buses and lorries from which it had gained fifteen years experience before the grouping. However, 1923 was not the best of times for one part of the new group to extend experiments of that kind, so it was 1927 before an offer from Beardmore (previously linked as a supplier to the LNWR) was considered. Beardmore had developed a diesel engine for use on airships (combining lightness and high rpm) which was quite remarkable for that period. One 500hp engine was fitted to a four coach set from the Manchester area electric section and English Electric transmission was accommodated. Thus was formed an early diesel electric by simply providing an energy source within an electric train unit.

The set spent ten months on test in the Fylde area where the terrain is fairly flat, but even there, the power to weight ratio of $3\frac{1}{2}$hp per ton proved inadequate. Tests were undertaken in parallel with normal steam push and pull, but even with one man operation, the running costs of the normal train were five pence per mile less than the diesel-electric. The new technology stretched the knowledge of the engineers considerably and breakdowns were common. Many dark hours were spent repairing working parts for the following day's service but at the end of the period, the unit had only managed to be in service on 32% of working days. So it was that the power unit was returned to the makers and the train broken up in 1928.

Therefore, if truth be told, it seems safe to state that nothing much of long-lasting significance emerged from the last twenty or so years of the pre-group period in the internal combustion field — and nothing at all until about ten years after grouping, at which point the final British attempts to marry conventional road technology to the needs of rail transport were attempted. These were mostly of LMS inspiration and the involvement of this company might just have been influenced by the successful introduction of internal combustion on the 3ft gauge County Donegal Railways system in Ireland, where the LMS (as post-1922 successor to the Midland) had a joint interest.

Whatever, in mainland Britain, the LMS started in 1932 in conjunction with the Michelin tyre company of France. In these experiments, the shock-absorbing properties of pneumatic tyres, mentioned above, were to be made the justification for evaluating ultra-lightweight construction, for the vehicles were designed in such a way that rubber tyres actually ran on the rail

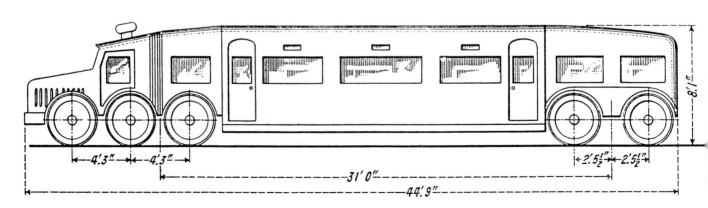

The three LMS Leyland railcars appeared in 1933 (Nos.29950-2) and this, the only known official view, shows the first example when new. Its neat lines were thoroughly in the contemporary motor bus idiom and the livery was crimson lake and cream, the roof (initially), probably being pale grey or white. The 40 seats were all third class and the cars were first used in the Accrington, Blackburn, Lower Darwen, Preston and Hamilton districts in turn, their later usage not being known. (LMS Official)

surface, thus replacing the normal steel tyres and leaving the steel flange to do its normal task. The first example, entirely French built and known as 'La Micheline', was a ten-wheel vehicle entirely in the road-coach stylistic idiom but far more luxuriously appointed than anything hitherto seen. It seated only 24, but was almost 45ft long and yet at 5 tons it was very light in weight for a railway vehicle. It had carpeted floors, a mixture of armchairs and conventionally transverse seats and was tested between Bletchley and Oxford in 1932.

At much the same time, the AEC company managed to persuade both the GWR and LNER to trial a conventional AEC 'Regal' single deck motor bus, an excellent contemporary design, with rail wheels substituted for the road wheels and with a fixed front axle. It ran between Slough and Reading (GWR) and also in the Hatfield area (LNER) but nothing much came of it save for a quantity of rather exaggeratedly favourable publicity! And, of course, the GWR came up with a far better solution only a few years later as Chapter 5 will reveal.

A year later, a trio of four-wheel railbuses was built for the LMS by Leyland Motors. They seated 40, weighed only 10 tons and were symmetrical end-to-end about their centreline, whereon were positioned the outer doors. They had transverse

seats facing outwards from the centre of the cars whose enclosed bodywork was of characteristic bus style. They were yet again an example of the pure road vehicle approach in terms of the method of getting direct drive to the wheels and appear to have been rather more successful than most, surviving until 1951. They may even have had some slight influence on early BR four-wheel railbus experiments a few years later, but in general their effect was minimal.

Soon after this, in 1934 and in conjunction with Karrier Motors Ltd. of Huddersfield, the LMS returned to rather more orthodox road vehicle technology but in a quite revolutionary way — a fascinating attempt to provide a genuine dual purpose vehicle rather than try to adapt an existing road design for rail use only. The idea was to produce a unit which could run

This view of 'La Micheline', believed to be at Oxford, was taken in 1932. It is offered together with a contemporary drawing, from which the general characteristics of this unusual vehicle can readily be appreciated, though it must be said that the drawing does not accord entirely with the reality of the car itself, for reasons the writer has been unable to discover. Note particularly the great length, compared with the low (24) seating capacity — hence, presumably, the articulation. Other than its first trials between Oxford and Bletchley, little seems to be on record about the subsequent history of this unique car. (T. J. Edgington Collection)

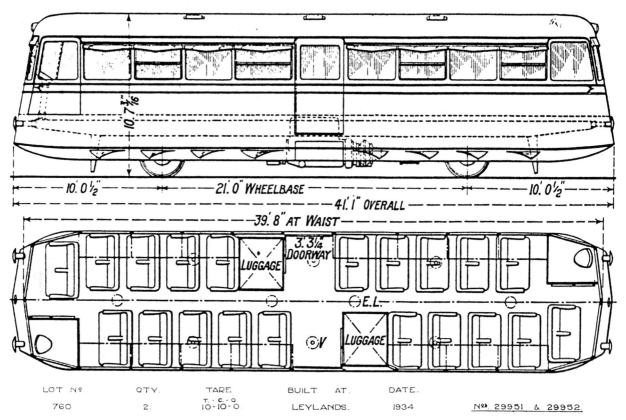

LOT №	QTY.	TARE.	BUILT AT.	DATE.	
760	2.	T. C. O 10-10-0	LEYLANDS.	1934	№ 29951 & 29952.

Leyland Railbus for the LMS. Scale: 4mm = 1ft

either on road or rail and the outcome was the celebrated but never duplicated 'Ro-Railer'. This was so logical and obvious a concept that even now one wonders why it was not pursued with more vigour; it would surely have had many useful applications even in more modern circumstances. Not much more than half the length of 'La Micheline', it actually seated two more people (26) but there was a 2 ton weight penalty compared with the French design.

The episode is well recorded, thus needing but brief mention here, but in essence involved a conventional single deck motor bus, little modified in basic appearance save for entrance doors on both sides to suit the 'rail' mode, which was fitted with both road and rail wheels. In 'road' configuration, the railway wheels, being smaller in diameter, simply rotated idly out of harm's way behind the road wheels but on transfer to rail, the steering was 'locked' and, with the road wheels raised by

means of eccentrics between wheel hub and rim, the unit became a railcar. The modal transfer took only two or three minutes and one of the unit's more celebrated uses was between Stratford-upon-Avon and the nearby LMS Welcombe Hotel. Maybe it was too small for more widespread use, who knows, but like so many other ideas it withered on the branch. That said, little more seems to have been recorded of this experiment than that of 'La Micheline'; maybe both were too limited in their scope or too low in seating capacity.

But the next pneumatic tyred experiment was an altogether more ambitious affair. Sponsored by Armstrong-Siddeley Motors Ltd., who provided the engine unit, the LMS, in 1935, introduced a 56 seat Michelin railcar onto its Oxford-Cambridge service. The car itself was the standard Michelin 16-wheel type (two eight-wheel bogies with a raised 'turret' driving cab) and represented a concept already quite well

The celebrated LMS 'Ro-Railer' at Stratford-upon-Avon. The letterboard on the side reads: "Blisworth Stratford & Welcombe Hotel", the only recorded regular service which it performed. It was painted LMS crimson lake with a white (cream?) roof and locomotive-type lettering, apparently applied by hand rather than by the usual company transfers. It was never, so far as is known, given a running number other than its road vehicle registration identity: UR 7924.
(Pendragon Collection)

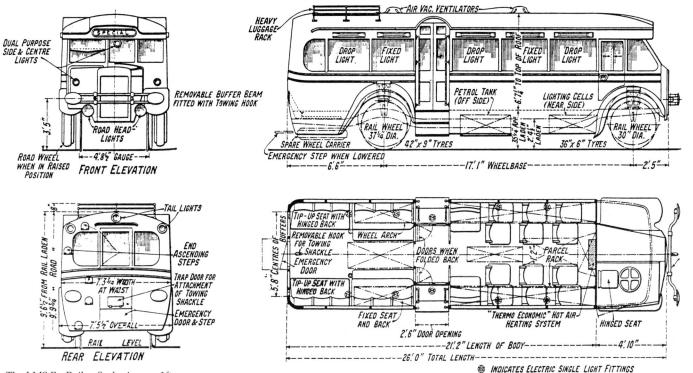

The LMS Ro-Railer. Scale: 4mm = 1ft

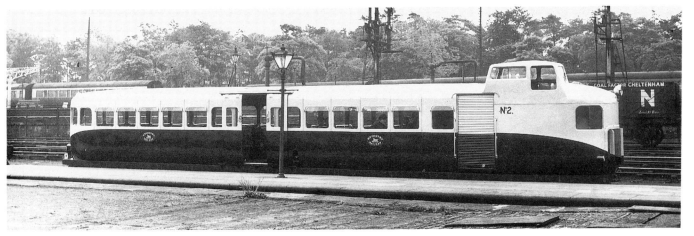

The second pneumatic tyred railcar to be tried by the LMS: Michelin Car No.2 at Leamington Spa (Avenue) station in 1937. It was inscribed 'Coventry Car' and the No.2 may well have been related to the earlier 'La Micheline' which never, so far as is known, carried a number. Sponsored by Armstrong-Siddeley in 1935, it clearly had a longer spell in traffic than most of the other experimental cars of the period but was never in LMS ownership. The livery is not known but was probably red and cream. (G. Coltas Collection)

known in France. Its trial performance was impressive: nearly 70mph in almost total silence. It weighed in at little more than 8 tons and its seating capacity was fully comparable with other contemporary railcars but, yet again, no-one seems to have been impressed enough to cause the LMS — or anyone else for that matter — to repeat the idea. Curiously, ever since then, the French have always found some application for pneumatic tyred railway vehicles, best known these days in the context of some lines on the Paris Metro; but then there are those who would argue that in the 20th Century, French engineers have usually been ahead of the British in the purely railway context — look at their altogether more positive reaction to Euro Tunnel, for example!

In the British context, therefore, the emergence of internal combustion in a truly significant form still had some way to go; but before then, we need to turn back to steam.

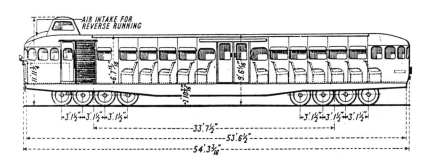

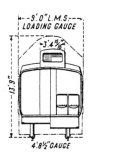

56 SEATS

Contemporary diagram (not to scale) of the Michelin 16-wheel railcar

Chapter Four

A SECOND CHANCE FOR STEAM

IN THE FIRST QUARTER OF THE CENTURY, British technology had not really produced any sort of lasting answer for the 'middle ground' type of services mentioned at the start of this survey and it was only after the 1923 grouping that railway engineers at last began to come up with ideas which gave better prospect of success. They did not all work, of course, and some distinctly comical ideas came and went, almost without trace; but overall, there were some forward moves and even the relative failures were not without their own bizarre interest as the last chapter revealed. In consequence, it was an interesting time for those who studied these things and though we may now smile at some of the ideas on offer, it is just as well to recall that they were propounded in all seriousness as a genuine attempt to solve very real problems.

Regardless of propulsion, the favoured solution nearly always took the shape of a light railcar and the basic purposes for which they were most suited were best summarised in an article in *The Railway Engineer* for April 1934:

a) To meet road competition in sparsely populated districts.
b) To develop branch line traffic.
c) To pick up and distribute between main line junctions.
d) To provide economical high speed inter-urban services for light loads.

There were still only two likely sources of motive power to be tapped: steam and internal combustion. Both enjoyed rather more success in the 1920s and 1930s than the earlier examples had done and the first of these forms the basis of this chapter.

As we have seen, the Edwardian steam railmotors mostly came and went like butterflies in summer and the 1920s dawned with little forward progress, save for electrification where the high initial infrastructure cost could be justified — hardly a relevant issue in the area we are discussing. Even so, and allowing that most of the early internal combustion experiments went much the same way as the majority of Edwardian steam cars, it would have been a brave soul indeed, who could have predicted that steam would have a second, rather more successful 'bite at the cherry' during the 1920s and 1930s; yet such it was, mainly due to the persistence of but one of the 'Big Four' companies, the LNER.

The LNER was in many ways the most poverty stricken of the Big Four. It had some good routes but its industrial hinterland probably suffered more from the depression, relative to the whole system, than did that of its rivals and this may have been a part cause. Whatever the reasons, soon after the grouping, the LNER began to take a very serious interest in a new form of steam railcar developed by the Sentinel Waggon Works Ltd in association with Cammell Laird & Co. Ltd. This went with a renewed assessment of the role of the railcar and it will help briefly to discuss this aspect before going onto the cars themselves.

Traditionally, the older type of steam railcar had suffered from two main faults: it was generally seen as merely replacing existing and more expensive conventional trains and, for the most part, its construction kept too closely to design practices associated with conventional stock. The result of this was that it rarely improved the service frequency and even where it was successful in attracting traffic, it was either too feeble to cope with it or, if made more powerful, did not show the hoped for cost savings. Many railways therefore resorted to the push-pull option, using conventional locomotives and coaches.

The new approach to railcars started from the rather different presumption that, properly designed, a railcar need not simply replace existing trains — of which only a few per day might have run — but actually provide a better service by operating more frequently. This would reduce the need to add vehicles to a powered unit which was self-evidently incapable of pulling them (as had often been tried, usually without success), but instead, by the simple expedient of operating more railcars, offer greater service frequency by way of compensation.

Interestingly, as I pen these words, this very policy has fairly recently proved the main cause for increased patronage in many areas of Britain, not least in my own 'back yard' so to speak. The introduction of four-wheel 'Pacer' railcars on the West Yorkshire Metropolitan area during the 1980s — more widely too for that matter — allowed, for example, an hourly service from Leeds to York via Harrogate and half-hourly to Harrogate and Knaresborough. Although the cars were and are pretty dire in comfort terms, and by no means free from mechanical and other problems, their introduction has effectively killed off the Harrogate-York bus competition and provided better local services from both Harrogate and Knaresborough to the two bigger cities than the steam trains, or even the first generation DMUs during their time had ever managed to do.

However, to do this in the steam context, just as in the modern day, meant using a vehicle which, owing to its lightness and simplicity, needed a smaller and less complicated power unit than was offered by the conventional locomotive style of construction. It was a tricky balancing act, as BR have more recently found with these self-same 'Pacer' trains, because railway vehicles need to be much stronger than the road equivalent, thus risking a weight penalty, but the Sentinel-Cammell steam railcars were a very fine attempt.

The very first of them was put to work in 1923 on the Jersey Railways & Tramways Ltd. in the Channel Islands, an unlikely enough location but one which gave to this long-closed narrow-gauge system an interesting and by no means insignificant footnote in railway history. But it was its espousal by the LNER which was to be the significant breakthrough. In 1924, trials were conducted in Durham and North Yorkshire of a slightly more powerful version of the Jersey car and later, of another car with larger boiler. The outcome seems to have been successful, for in 1925, two Sentinel cars were purchased and put to use in East Anglia to operate between Norwich and Lowestoft and from King's Lynn to Hunstanton. They incorporated the bodies of the original trial cars and were of lightweight construction and rather low-slung appearance. Unlike all other LNER Sentinels, they entered service without conventional drawgear and did not reveal the prominent solebar below the bodysides which was characteristic of all the later cars.

Two years later, two more cars were acquired of rather more substantial construction which added just over six tons to the weight. These were the first to have proper drawgear and visible solebars and 1928 was to see another 20 of this more robust design added to the fleet, giving a total of 24 cars of what was, in effect, the 'first generation' Sentinel type. In 1929 and 1930, the two lightweight pioneers were rebuilt (each slightly differently) to be more nearly like the later vehicles and one of them acquired drawgear in the process, though both retained their original 'low' styling. Although the full story of this LNER experiment (in fact, it was rather more than this) has been well

The first LNER 'Lightweight' Sentinel, No.43306, at Doncaster works on 17th September 1938. Dating from 1925, this car ran as No.12E and was one of only two LNER cars built in the low height configuration. As seen here, it reveals the proper drawgear equipment fitted during the 1930 rebuild — see text. Along with its 'partner' (No.13E later 43307), it was one of only three LNER Sentinels never to carry a name, though why this was so is uncertain, and it was withdrawn in April 1940.
(T. J. Edgington Collection)

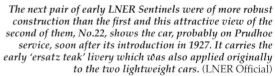

The next pair of early LNER Sentinels were of more robust construction than the first and this attractive view of the second of them, No.22, shows the car, probably on Prudhoe service, soon after its introduction in 1927. It carries the early 'ersatz teak' livery which was also applied originally to the two lightweight cars. (LNER Official)

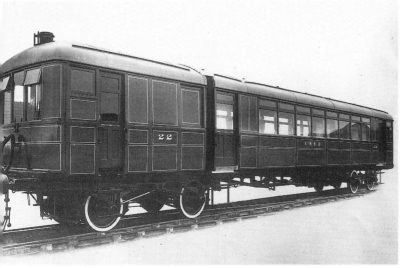

Opposite side view of LNER Sentinel No.22 when new. This was the last of the type to be given 'teak' livery and in 1929 was named Brilliant *and repainted red and cream, both changes being in line with the late 1927 LNER decision to name all the new railcars and paint them in brighter colours.*
(Pendragon Collection)

The LMS, though generally less attracted to Sentinels than the LNER, made more use of the lightweight 'low height' cars and this well known official view at Ripley shows the first of them undergoing trials on 12th March 1925. It later became No.2232 in the LMS lists, being renumbered 29900 in 1933 and withdrawn in 1937. (LMS Official)

recorded — see Bibliography — their importance also merits reasonably detailed treatment here.

Basically, these first cars made use of a standard boiler and engine unit also used in the well-known Sentinel steam road wagons. This was a proven and economical power unit and was fitted inside a cab unit articulated to the main passenger portion of the railcar. The engine itself was of two cylinder double-acting configuration and drive to the wheels was by two chains to the rear axle from the sprockets at the end of the crankshaft. All had vertical boilers but the first two cars had the engine part set horizontally in their original state. On rebuilding, this vas altered to the vertical engine arrangement of the later and heavier cars of 1927 and 1928.

The two lightweights of 1925 and the first two heavier cars in 1927 were finished in ersatz 'teak', fully panelled, but the final 20 were given the striking red and cream livery of the former NER electrics, reflecting the fact that all were put to work on former NER territory. Before much longer, both schemes were abandoned in favour of a green and cream livery which most who remember them at all will no doubt recall. This series of Sentinels also introduced the LNER 'naming' tradition for its railcars, old stage coach names being the most common single theme.

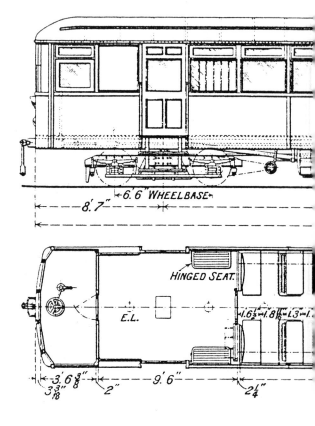

However, before continuing the LNER story, mention must be made of the fact that at much the same time as the LNER was conducting its tests on these new style railcars, the LMS also tried them out. In 1925, trials were conducted with a hired prototype on the Ripley Branch and a fleet of thirteen cars (the prototype plus a production batch of twelve) was put in service during 1926-7, a year or so ahead of the main LNER order. The LMS cars were all of lightweight low-slung design with less of the working parts exposed below the frames and no conventional drawgear. They were unnamed and finished in standard lined crimson lake livery.

Like the original LNER lightweights, they were slightly shorter and one foot narrower than the later LNER cars and the appended drawings of the LMS Sentinels can be taken as

This second view of the first LMS Sentinel (now in company ownership) shows the car in service at Perth in 1932. Though generally recorded as being No.2233 in most sources, examination of the running number on the original print under magnification shows No.2232 clearly inscribed. This may have been a paintshop error, but since ex-MR railcar No.2233 was still (officially) in stock, it may well be correct. The somewhat unkempt nature of the car hints that it may not have been altogether well regarded! (T. J. Edgington Collection)

broadly characteristic of both lightweight types. But they were not quite identical as the appended pictures reveal. The LMS cars had only 44 seats and a slightly over 21T tare weight whereas the LNER lightweights were quoted with 52 seats at 17T tare. For comparison, the later and heavier LNER chain driven cars were almost 26T except for the 1927 pair (just over 23T)

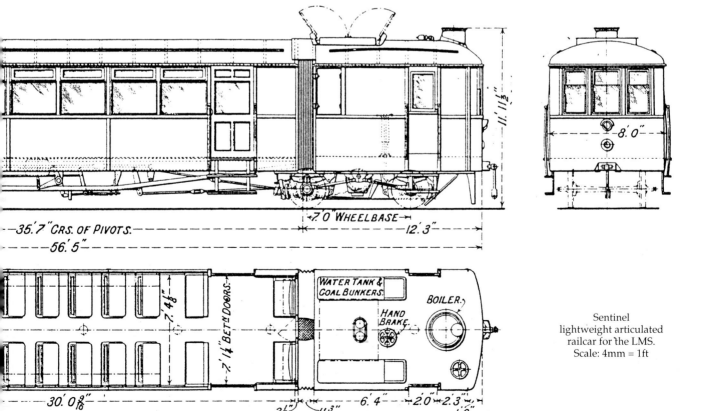

Sentinel
lightweight articulated
railcar for the LMS.
Scale: 4mm = 1ft

A rare view of two LMS Sentinels, believed Nos.29907/11, in company with ex-MR Class 2 0-6-0 No.3420 inside Wigston Shed on 5th November 1934. By now, the LMS Sentinels mostly had less than a year left to go and the poor outward state of the cars suggests that there was little useful work for them to do.
(T. J. Edgington Collection)

In both versions of the articulated Sentinels of both companies, interiors were very similar. In the lightweight cars (only 8ft wide) seats were arranged 2 + 2 and on the later 9ft wide cars 2 + 3. Both had reversible 'walk over' seat backs and mahogany interior finish, LMS seats being dark green and those in the LNER cars being quoted as having 'standard LNER pattern' material.

Subsequent events were to demonstrate that these Sentinel-Cammell railcars were to be the definitive steam type, but before considering their development in later years, it is helpful to keep the chronology in order by returning to the LNER and introducing its second approach to the problem — a purchase of the rival type offered by Messrs Clayton Wagons Ltd. of Lincoln, the LNER evaluation being conducted more or less in parallel with that of the first Sentinel cars.

The Clayton cars originated in 1925, originally for use in New Zealand, and in 1927, the LNER acquired one (as also, simultaneously did the Egyptian State Railways) for test purposes. Again, the company was reasonably satisfied and a production order for ten more was placed in 1928. In these cars, road vehicle practice was again adopted but since the power unit was differently conceived, it made quite a noticeable difference to the configuration of the powered end.

They used essentially the same standard engine and boiler unit as fitted to Clayton 'undertype' road wagons. This unit, like the chain-driven Sentinels, also employed a two cylinder layout but the totally enclosed engine, mounted above the leading axle of the driving bogie, drove the wheels by a crankshaft pinion in connection with a spur wheel on the axle. The driving bogie wheels were then connected by outside coupling rods attached in conventional locomotive fashion. The centre of the power bogie carried a conventional bogie bolster and pivot, to which was fixed the leading end of the car body. This placed the boiler within the body but left the coal bunker and water tanks in full view ahead of the bodywork. It was thus, in effect, a rigid railcar with a pivoting power bogie, partly exposed to view. The visual effect was mildly comical.

Like the Sentinels, the first LNER Clayton car was finished in 'teak' livery, the main order mostly being delivered in red and cream. All eventually ended up with green and cream livery and were again named after stage coaches. The last of the series, a 44 seater with 'more comfortable'(!) bucket seats and a few technical refinements, wore green and cream livery from the outset and helped to establish this style. It carried the wonderfully ambiguous name *Bang Up*(!).

As things turned out, the LNER seems to have decided to concentrate on the Sentinel alternative very soon after it had put its Claytons into service, but this may also have had something to do with the fact that Clayton Wagons Ltd went into liquidation in 1929, thus complicating the matter of spares. The fact that maintenance of the Clayton cars became an increasing problem (the first to be declared unfit for further traffic was withdrawn as early as 1932) was not discovered until after the LNER had already determined on a much larger fleet of Sentinels (which in hindsight must have seemed a sensible decision) but there may have been 'writing on the wall' at a much earlier date.

At all events, 1928 saw the ordering of by far the biggest batch of new steam railcars ever placed by a British railway company. They were all Sentinels and derived from an experimental 'one-off' new design, tested early in 1928 and eventually taken into LNER stock and named *Integrity*. This car remained unique for, meantime, Sentinel had continued to develop the gear drive with yet another trial car and the LNER prudently waited to place its larger order until this developed type had been subjected to satisfactory tests — duly made. This car became No.2133 *Nettle* and was, in effect, the prototype of the standard series which the LNER procured in some quantity. *Integrity*, meantime, went into the main LNER number series as No.2135, remaining a 'one-off'. continued on page 54

Interior views of the Sentinel railcars are few and far between but this official picture gives a very clear impression of the LNER arrangement in a 2 + 3 seating configuration. It is almost certainly one of the two original 'heavyweights' of 1927, probably No.22, though some sources give it as one of the first rigid cars Nettle. *The LMS 2 + 2 seating was much the same as seen here — ie mahogany framing with 'throw-over' seat backs but with plain upholstery in dark green.* (LNER Official)

The two duotone liveries adopted by the LNER after 1927 can be difficult to tell apart in a black and white source unless the date is precisely known as in this official view of car No.22 Brilliant, immediately after receiving its name and being repainted from 'teak' in January 1929. (LNER Official)

Right:
A charming study of No.41, the first Clayton railcar in service at Lintz Green, County Durham and about to work the 2.13pm to Newcastle in August 1927, a month after its introduction. It was the only Clayton car to sport the 'teak' livery and was also unique in having the luggage compartment at the rear. It was named Pilot *and painted red and cream in March 1929 and withdrawn from service in September 1936.*
(Pendragon Collection)

Clayton railcar No.296 Wonder, *seen here brand new in 1928 in red/cream livery, typified the main production series of Claytons, all but the last of which emerged in this livery — see text. They were a foot longer with a slightly shorter luggage area, now at the front, with four extra seats in consequence — set longitudinally adjacent to the entrance door. It is also worth noting that Clayton cars had most of the seats arranged in facing pairs forming six bays of ten. Other small differences (eg oval buffers and a sun vizor above the driver's end window) may also be noted. It was withdrawn in September 1936. (LNER Official)*

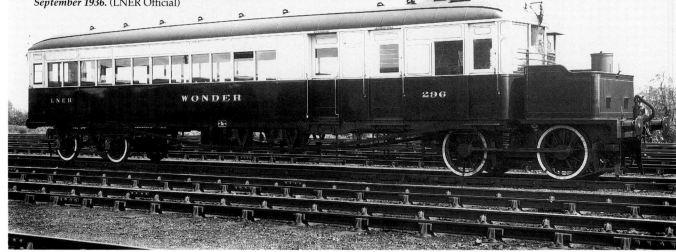

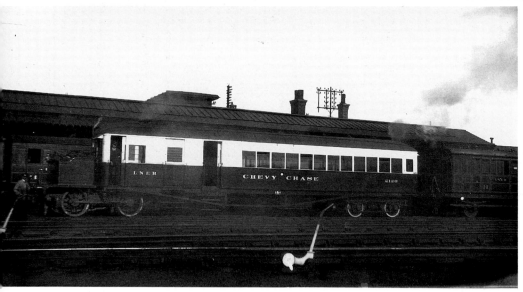

Opposite side view of Clayton car No.2120 Chevy Chase, *believed taken at Doncaster. It shows the car in red/cream livery and with its very short-lived first number; it became No.42 in the same month it was built (June 1928) and No.43302 in 1934. It was one of five to last until 1937, being withdrawn in February of that year.* (Pendragon Collection)

The bunkers of the Clayton railcars had a tendency to spill coal so it was not long before coal rails were introduced: August 1928 onwards. Two basic styles were apparent, one as shown here (following the bunker contour) and used in the Southern area; the other having a straight top and lower front end 'in-fill' and used in the NE. There were differences in detail (eg two or three rails with round or rectangular section). The example illustrated No.43305 Transit, *had the more usual three rails but of the relatively less common rectangular cross-section. The picture was almost certainly taken when the car was about to be broken up after withdrawal in February 1937 and shows the green/cream livery. Built in June 1928 as No.2121, the car was renumbered 6199 two months later and received its final number in August 1934. (NRM Collection)*

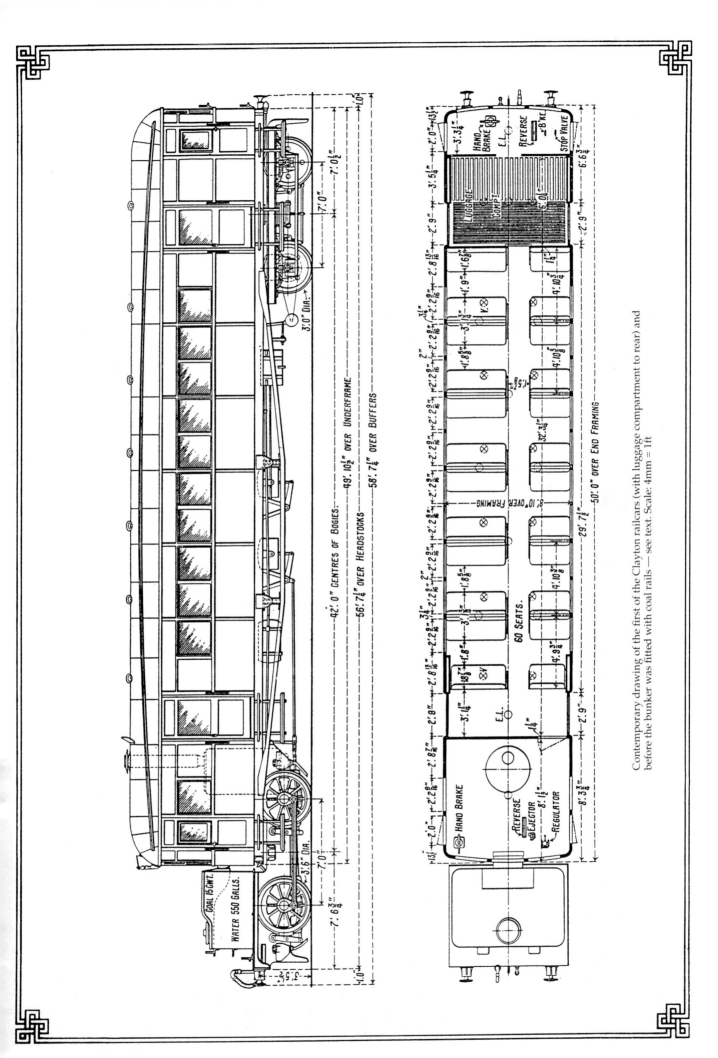

Contemporary drawing of the first of the Clayton railcars (with luggage compartment to rear) and before the bunker was fitted with coal rails — see text. Scale: 4mm = 1ft

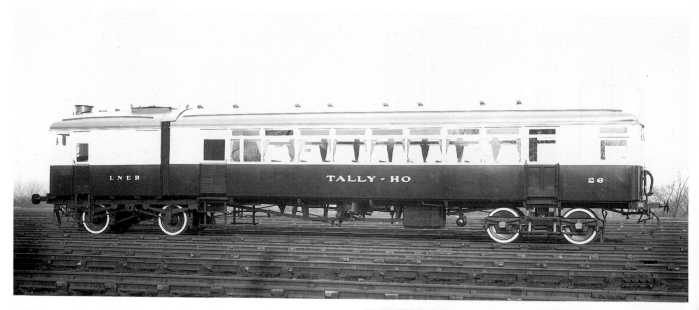

Tally Ho **was the first of the production series of articulated Sentinels and also the first to get red and cream livery as shown in this official ex-works January 1928 view. All remaining articulated Sentinels came into service in this colour scheme, the last being delivered in May 1928. But no sooner had this happened than one of the experimental rigid cars (Nettle — see text) was painted green and cream which established a new livery into which all the articulated cars were eventually repainted from May 1930 onwards.** Tally Ho *was finally withdrawn in August 1945.* (LNER Official)

It is possible that these cars were Sentinel's response to Clayton (whose imminent liquidation may not have been apparent at the time), for not only did they employ gear drive but they were mounted on a rigid chassis, the steam and exhaust pipes having flexible joints to allow for the differential movement of the engine portion (mounted direct to the power bogie) and the boiler unit (fixed to the main chassis). *Integrity* made use of the existing two-cylinder power unit which led, in turn to the revised version with six-cylinder single acting engine employing gear and cardan shaft drive of which *Nettle* and her eighteen half-sisters were the first examples.

Between 1928 and 1931, but mostly during 1928 and 1929, no fewer than 50 of these new six-cylinder railcars were eventually obtained, 49 for the LNER and one for the Axholme Joint Railway (LMS/LNER), later taken over by the LNER in 1933. They were undoubtedly the most successful Sentinel design and went into service in many areas though, as usual, the greater number went to the by now traditional ex-NER territory. Stage coach names were again favoured but this time, a few specifically regional titles were also employed. Four similar cars were provided for the CLC in 1929, none of them named.

Legally, the Axholme car was owned by the LMS until 1933 (although it was painted green and cream) and was some three feet longer than the otherwise similar LNER cars. Its allocated number (44) was in the pre-1933 LMS carriage series and it was also designated LMS 1933 series No.29987 — not carried. The LMS also owned another rigid Sentinel — a solitary example built in 1930. But, as with its articulated contemporaries, it was to a slightly different design than the LNER equivalent, this time rather lighter in weight (25t compared with 28t 15cwt). It spent most of its time in Scotland but, like all the other LMS Sentinels, did not enjoy as long an active life as the LNER examples.

The LNER rigid railcar purchase was completed in 1930 and 1932 with five more Sentinels in two separate batches, each

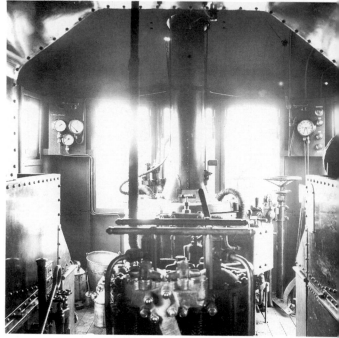

The interior of the boiler room of Tally Ho *when built. The coal bunkers, carried internally, were re-filled through overhead doors towards the rear of this compartment but not readily seen on this view.* Tally Ho *was also interesting in having a larger chimney than the others because it housed a spark arrester at first, removed in December 1929.* (LNER Official)

embodying a beefed-up 12-cylinder engine configuration for the more hilly NE Yorkshire coast routes. In fact, two sets of standard six-cylinder power units were used, each driving one of the two bogies. There were technical changes between the batches and the passenger accommodation was reduced from the customary 59: first to 54 and then to 48, the latter being in 2 + 2 'luxury' configuration. Finally, mention should also be made of the solitary 'twin' Sentinel: *Phenomena* of 1930. This had two passenger 'cars', articulated at the centre and it too had 12-cylinder propulsion, this time with the two 'engines' driving the leading and central bogies. The powered end seated 39 and the 'trailer' portion, 83.

Talking of trailers to run with railcars, the LNER procured some singularly unlovely four-wheel examples of the genre in

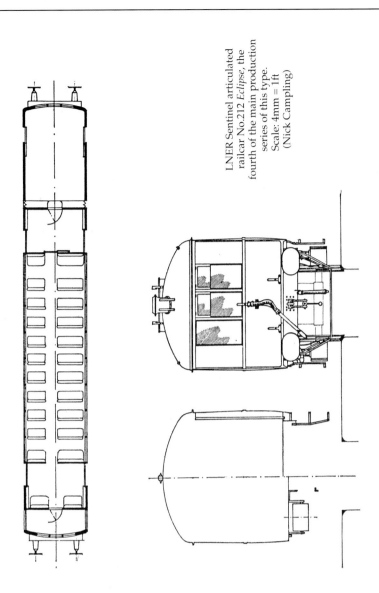

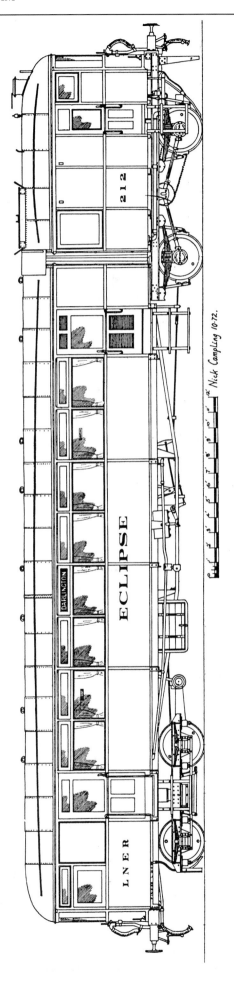

LNER Sentinel articulated railcar No.212 *Eclipse*, the fourth of the main production series of this type. Scale: 4mm = 1ft (Nick Campling)

1929 from Claytons. Classed as 'Trailer Brake Thirds', eight only were built and never seem to have been very popular. Pictures of them in use are somewhat rare and little is on record of their working life; they were all withdrawn between March 1948 and March 1949.

In terms of usefulness in service, the LNER railcars clearly had a longer innings than most of the pre-1914 steam railmotors and its fleet of 91 units from all sources (92 counting the former Axholme car) must have effected quite substantial savings during the 15-20 years when they were operational. The Claytons were the shortest lived, faring no better than the Edwardian steam railmotors, maybe for much the same reasons, and mostly went out of service during 1936-7. But the Sentinels lasted rather better.

The 12-cylinder cars were not too long-lived but the two bigger batches mostly served until the mid-1940s, many until after the war. One of them, No. 2136 *Hope* just reached BR. Withdrawn early in 1948 it would have been a worthy candidate for preservation but its name was maybe too symbolic of the whole story of the steam railcar. The fact is that none of them actually gave 20 years of revenue service and although on average they did rather better than the Edwardian steam railmotors, the final examples of the latter (ex-LYR and LNWR — see Chapter 2), which also lasted until the late 1940s, had enjoyed a far longer working life. As for the LMS Sentinels, they lasted less than ten years!

This fine view of No.225 True Blue *by an anonymous photographer was taken at Hartlepool shed with the destination board reading 'The Hartlepools'. The car was red and cream at the time and, indeed, was one of the last two of this type to keep this livery, the other being* Trafalgar *(both repainted in March 1931). The picture gives a useful visual clue because the side destination boards were replaced on the NE area cars from October 1929 (nine months before the livery change) by roller blind indicators; so if a picture reveals a side indicator board on a NE area car, it is red and cream.* True Blue *was withdrawn in December 1942. (Pendragon Collection)*

Together, the LNER and LMS Sentinels were broadly equivalent (numerically) to the earlier generation GWR railcars (Chapter 2), albeit rather more variable in detail configuration. The writer is unable to state which of the solutions gave a better economic return, though maybe the advantage lay with the GWR if only because most of its railcars had a considerably extended lease of life in the form of auto-trailers, a solution which never, so far as the writer can appraise, seems to have been considered with the Sentinels or Claytons. However, both types were important in the continuing evolution of ideas. The accompanying table gives a chronology of both the LNER/LMS Sentinels and Claytons by way of summary and a comprehensive series of annotated drawings and diagrams of the major variants is also offered.

continued on page 67

CHRONOLOGY OF LNER AND LMS SENTINEL AND CLAYTON STEAM RAILCARS/TRAILERS

Date of First Example	Number Built	For Whom	Maker and Type	Withdrawals		
				First	Last	Notes:
1925	2 #	LNER	Sentinel Lightweight Articulated *	1/40	4/40	Notes:
1926	13	LMS	Sentinel Lightweight Articulated *	1935	1937	
1927	2	LNER	Sentinel Articulated (prototype) *	12/42	2/44	# Rebuilt 1930
1927	20	LNER	Sentinel Articulated *	6/29 +	10/46	
1927	11	LNER	Clayton Railcar	7/32 +	2/37	* Chain Drive
1928	1	LNER	Sentinel Rigid (experimental) §		11/47	
1928	49	LNER	Sentinel Rigid §	2/43	2/48	+ Premature withdrawals
1929	4	CLC	Sentinel Rigid §	10/44	10/44	
1929	8	LNER	Clayton Trailer	3/48	3/49	§ Gear Drive
1930	1	LMS	Sentinel Rigid (for Axholme Jt) § @		7/44	
1930	1	LMS	Sentinel Rigid §		12/39	@ To LNER stock 1933
1930	2	LNER	Sentinel Rigid (twin engine) §	9/41	11/41	
1930	1	LNER	Sentinel Articulated Twin Car §		5/42	

Left and above:
The LNER Sentinels wandered far and wide and these views show No.226 Ebor *in red and cream at Cudworth on Kirk Smeaton (ex-Hull and Barnsley route) service in 1928 and in green and cream (note the replacement destination blind) at East Hartlepool in September 1933. The car was to be withdrawn earlier than most of its type in September 1939.* (T. J. Edgington Collection, Pendragon Collection)

Three articulated cars in an undated view at Botanic Gardens shed, Hull. Two still carry their original destination boards and all have brackets, so c.1929-30 and red/cream livery seems likely. Hull was one of the important locations for the early Sentinels, no fewer than five of the articulated series being initially sent there and the cars featured are, left to right: No.26 Tally Ho, *No.212* Eclipse *and No.29* Rockingham, *withdrawn in 1945, 1943 and 1944 respectively.* (Pendragon Collection)

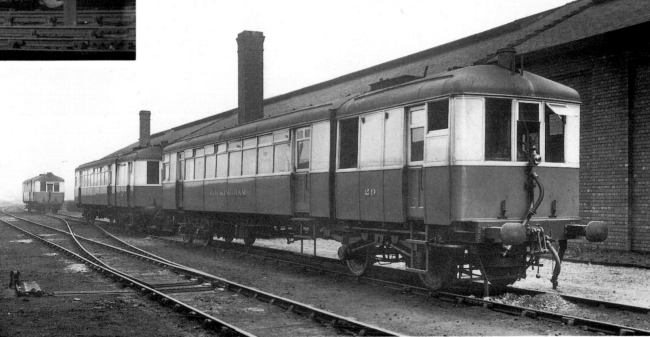

Above:
The experimental rigid chassis Sentinel of 1927 as LNER No.2135 Integrity at Newcastle Central in August 1932 in green and cream. This car was a 'one-off' since, although making use of the new gear drive rather than the chain drive of the articulated Sentinels, it retained the original two cylinder engine unit. It was also unique in being the only rigid Sentinel to receive red and cream livery before the new style was settled. Tested by the LNER in late 1927, its evaluation continued during the time when the production series of red/cream articulated cars came into service and was painted to match. It was purchased from Sentinel in June 1928, a month after the LNER had also bought the six-cylinder Nettle (see text). These two gear driven rigid chassis cars paved the way for the large production series of rigid body Sentinels. (T. J. Edgington Collection)

Right & opposite page:
The main production series of rigid Sentinels was based on a six-cylinder engine with gear drive first used on Nettle, the first example to emerge being No.31 Flower of Yarrow in November 1928. These official views were both taken at the time (although some sources state, incorrectly, that the front view shows Nettle). The livery is green and cream (applied to all new LNER Sentinels from this point onwards) and No.31 itself lasted until September 1943. (LNER Official)

This pleasant view shows the opposite side of one of the first production series of rigid chassis Sentinels, No.36 Royal Eagle leaving Edinburgh Waverley c.1934, probably for North Leith. By now, the car had been fitted with a metal grid to protect the saloon window nearest to the rear driving compartment. It also shows the replacement of the sliding window behind the boiler room door at the front with a metal sheet — a change which became standardised with the second series of cars of this type and was applied retrospectively to earlier cars. Royal Eagle was based at St Margaret's shed when new and the only Sentinel to remain there permanently, though joined by others from time to time. It was withdrawn in August 1946. (NRM Collection)

After twenty rigid Sentinels had been delivered (including Integrity and Nettle) by early 1929, a few slight changes were made with the rest of the series which came into service from August 1929 onwards. Mechanically the same, the cars showed some cosmetic changes, most obvious being a change of the sliding window behind the side door of the engine compartment to a shutter arrangement and the replacement of opening toplights with a fixed version combined with frameless droplights in alternate windows. The pull handles for these can just be seen on both these views which also show the different form of destination indicator used in the NE area compared with elsewhere on the LNER — see previous views. No.38 Pearl (labelled for Stirling and based there at the time) shows the traditional solid board while No.2242 Cornwallis, a Hull Botanic Gardens car, has the NE area destination blind (marked for the Beverley service). The cars both came into service in late 1929 and were scrapped in April 1947 and June 1946 respectively. (Pendragon Collection — 2)

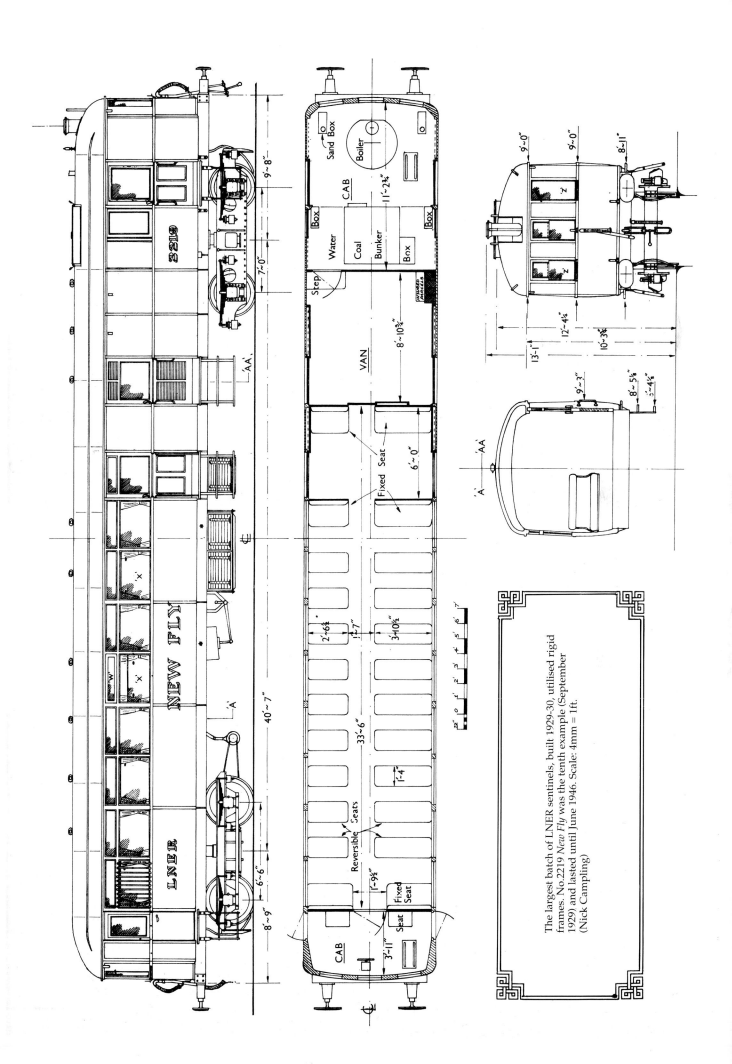

The largest batch of LNER sentinels, built 1929-30, utilised rigid frames. No.2219 *New Fly* was the tenth example (September 1929) and lasted until June 1946. Scale: 4mm = 1ft. (Nick Campling)

In 1942, instructions were given to paint all LNER Sentinels in dark brown livery when next due for repaint. It is unlikely that all were so treated — many being withdrawn in the later years of the war and afterwards in the green and cream style. No.2231 *Swift* was one of the exceptions, being seen here at Darlington Bank Top in 1947, from whence it was withdrawn in July of that year, by which time it was one of only four surviving Sentinels in LNER stock. (T. J. Edgington Collection)

Centre:
Four of the 1929 order for Sentinels were destined for the Cheshire Lines Committee, but did not receive the revised fixed toplight plus droplight arrangement of the contemporary LNER cars. Originally finished in CLC teak livery, they were later painted buff and brown as shown in this less than perfect view of what is believed to be CLC No.600 at Southport Lord Street in the 1930s. Maintained at Gorton, all four CLC cars were withdrawn in 1944, three of them having been in store (unserviceable?) at Trafford Park since November 1941. (Pendragon Collection)

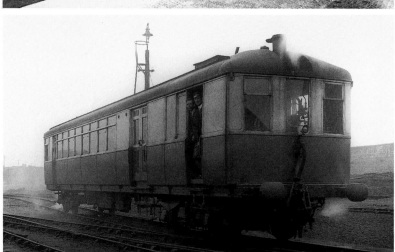

The solitary Sentinel for the Axholme Joint Railway (No.44), in spite of its green and cream livery, was actually owned by the LMS for a few years — see text. Built in late 1930, it was similar to the rest of the LNER rigid frame six-cylinder Sentinels in mechanical terms but its longer body had some detail differences which can be appreciated by comparing this view with those of the main series. Becoming LNER No.51915 in January 1934, it was not named and, after reconditioning at Gorton, went to work in the Lancashire area (amongst others) and is seen here at Lower Ince in May 1935. It was withdrawn in July 1944. (T. J. Edgington Collection)

The only rigid chassis Sentinel railcar to bear LMS colours was No.4349, renumbered 29913 in 1933. It was built in 1930 and is seen here in early days at Hamilton shed. Although generally similar in style to the main LNER series, there were some slight differences in the body arrangement, albeit rather subtle, which made it more akin to, though not exactly the same as, the Axholme Joint car. This view is of additional interest in showing the roof top coal doors open, seemingly a result of over-zealous re-fuelling. Later used on the Wanlockhead branch from Elvanfoot (ex-Caledonian), it was withdrawn in December 1939 and was the last LMS Sentinel to survive in service. (T. J. Edgington Collection)

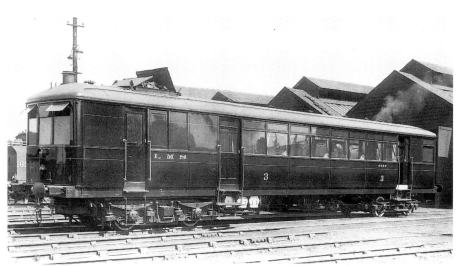

LNER No.2281 Old John Bull, *seen here when new, was one of two twin engine single cars built in 1930. To power the two engine units (one on each bogie), a larger boiler (a Woolnough marine type water tube unit) was used, which took up over six feet extra length. This was part compensated by an increase in overall underframe length to that of the Axholme Joint car — see earlier view — but still resulted in a reduced seating capacity. The coal bunker was also repositioned at the front of the engine compartment — note the rearward position of the chimney. There were, in consequence, only two front windows but otherwise, the styling followed that which had now become familiar on the large batch of single engine rigid frame Sentinels. Working from Middlesbrough together with its 'twin' (No.2283 Old Blue, stationed at Guisborough), it operated to Guisborough (originally as spare for Old Blue), but later on, both cars worked many other services in that rather hilly and twisting part of the old NER system. Both were withdrawn in 1941. (LNER Official)*

Below:
No.220 Defence *was the first of a trio of twin engined Sentinels which were to be the last LNER attempt to get more power out of a single unit car. They were even longer than the previous twin-engined cars but unlike them, the boiler was turned round with the chimney at the front and the coal bunker again at the rear. Even so, the larger nature of the boiler unit still caused the suppression of the central front window. There were other slight body changes as can be seen here and the cars were designed for that other hilly part of the NE coast in the Scarborough, Whitby and Saltburn areas (all allocated to Scarborough but one at each location). An innovation was to fit 2 + 2 'bucket' seats — this apparently classified them as 'luxury' cars! — which also resulted in a further drop in seating capacity. Built in 1932, they fared less well than even the other twin engine cars, being withdrawn between 1939 and 1941, Defence itself going in September 1940. (LNER Official)*

The solitary twin unit twin engine LNER Sentinel No.2291 Phenomena *was developed in 1930 in parallel with the first twin engined rigid cars and embodied a similar type of boiler and power bogies. Although articulation allowed the individual unit lengths to be reduced compared with a single unit car, a more than doubled carrying capacity was achieved with only a 25% increase in tare weight. It worked from South Blyth, the location of this view, taken soon after its introduction. Its higher seating capacity also made it very attractive for weekend excursion use. It lasted rather longer than the other twin engine Sentinels but not quite as long as the vast majority of the single engine cars (articulated or rigid) and it was withdrawn in May 1942.*
(LNER Official)

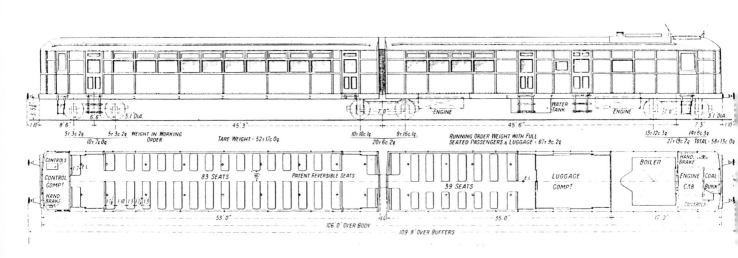

This official view of Sentinel No.2133 Cleveland *(built December 1928 and withdrawn October 1943) is one of very few pictures showing a Clayton trailer attached to a railcar of any kind. These trailers, of which No.2166 is the featured example, were very basic and their four-wheel chassis may well have affected their riding quality. (LNER Official)*

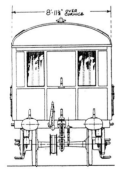

These interior views show the somewhat spartan nature of the eight trailer cars from Claytons, the occasional tip up seats in the luggage van being particularly unappealing. Perhaps the most interesting point to make is that the seats in the main part of the carriage followed the pattern of fixed bays, which the contemporary Clayton railcars also displayed, rather than the 'throw-over' type found in most Sentinels. (LNER Official — 2)

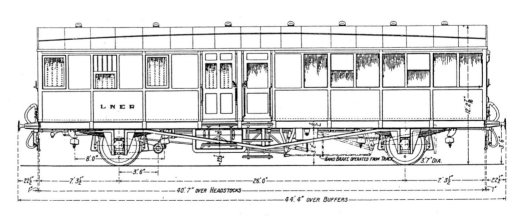

Clayton Trailer for the LNER steam railcars. Scale: 3mm = 1ft

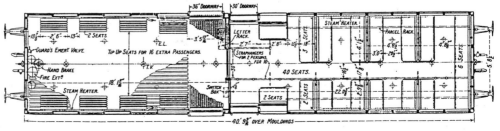

The strange 'torpedo' shape of the solitary Southern Railway Sentinel railcar is well shown in this side elevation taken when the car was new. It is offered in conjunction with a contemporary drawing of the car whose plan view clearly shows, from the cab arrangement at both ends, that it was designed for one man operation: the Devil's Dyke branch was very short and the nature of the machinery was such as to make it possible to stoke up for a complete trip at the start of each journey. (Pendragon Collection)

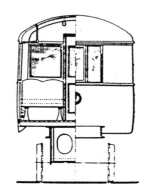

Scale of Drawing:
4mm = 1ft

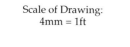

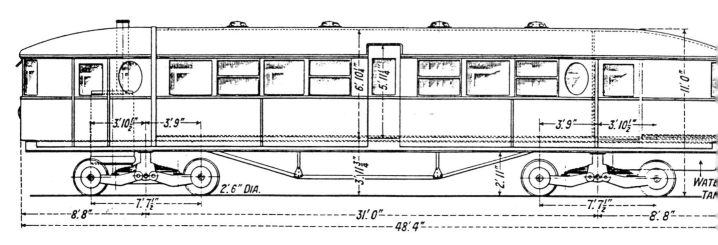

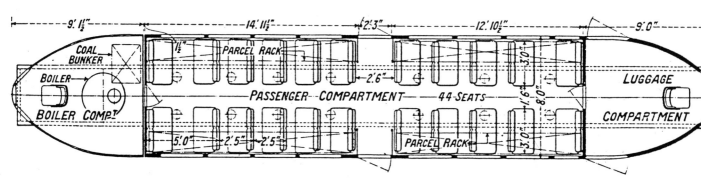

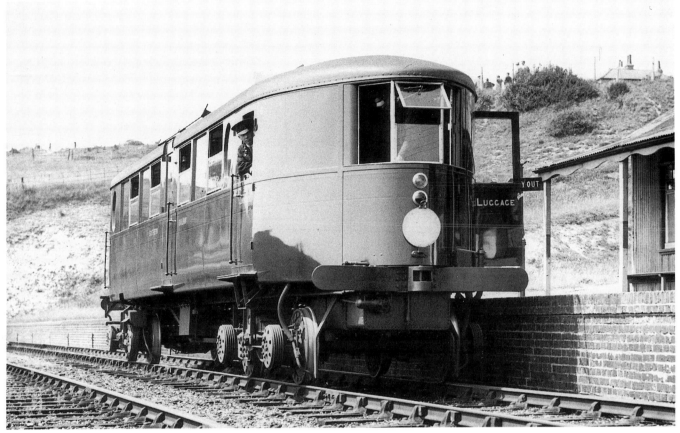

This second view of the Southern Railway Sentinel shows the car at The Dyke station during it brief period of operation. The primitive buffing gear adds to its almost toy-like appearance. (NRM Collection)

The steam railcar story was not quite finished in Britain with the building of the last LNER Sentinels in 1932, though it were well had it been so, for its final fling, a sort of Ruritanian creation built as a solo example for the Southern Railway was, in the writer's view, something of a tragic farce. Were its existence not confirmed photographically and elsewhere, it could well have been deemed a quaint flight of fancy doodled on the drawing board of an over-imaginative designer working for the tinplate toy makers of the day!

At much the same time as the SR was introducing its new electric services to Brighton in 1933, it put into operation a single Sentinel steam railcar on the steeply graded branch line from Hove to Devil's Dyke, high up in the South Downs north west of Brighton. This in itself would have made some sense: the branch was both steep and sharply curved; but instead of using one of the well-proved LNER type cars (or even the lighter weight LMS alternatives), the whole operation was made the excuse for creating a new sort of one-man operated bus unit. The engine part appears to have been a two-cylinder compound of unproven quality, slung on the driving axle and fed from a standard Sentinel type boiler fitted with a patent automatic stoker embodying a screw feed plus crusher.

It seemed a lot of technology to crack a very small nut and was then made even more bizarre by marrying it to a fashionably streamlined 'Zeppelin' type body which seemed to be perched on top as an afterthought. Maybe I am cruel but when

first I saw a picture of this extraordinary creation and realised that it was taken quite seriously on its introduction, I simply burst out laughing. It seems to to have survived until 1942, but actually ceased work in 1937. One cannot envisage even the unorthodox Oliver Bulleid seeing much merit in the thing and the fact that it was actually authorised by the normally rather conservative Richard Maunsell makes it all the more odd.

However, strange though it may seem, this was the very last self-propelled steam-powered passenger carrying rail vehicle devised for use in Britain and as such has its place in our story. But it only served to point out, along with the other Sentinels, Claytons and their railmotor ancestors, that as far as steam propulsion was concerned, the lightweight single unit was still not the full answer, even though the later generation steam railcars had made a better fist of it than most. If steam could still compete, then push-pull was the far better answer; meantime the jury was still out on the main issue.

Chapter Five

THE TRIUMPH OF THE DIESEL

TOWARDS THE END OF THE GENERALLY UNSUCCESSFUL British efforts to adapt road practice to railway use (Chapter 3), the early 1930s also saw the emergence of a few ideas wherein internal combustion engines were fitted to more 'railway-like' vehicles. This led to a further modest rash of experiments, the best of which continued with a form of direct drive propulsion. Of the others, one may, perhaps, single out for further mention those of Messrs Armstrong Whitworth in the diesel-electric field during 1931-3. These brought a new factor into the equation as far as Britain was concerned: the combination of a diesel engine and electric transmission of power to the wheels. In fact, neither the diesel nor the use of internal combustion for electricity generation were new in themselves and both had been tried independently in the British context, though never in dual harness as far as diesel powered railcars were concerned.

So far, all the internal combustion experiments reviewed (whether direct drive or via electric motors) had used petrol engines and this may well have been a partial cause of their usually less than successful outcome. As more modern experience has well and truly demonstrated, the compression-ignition engine, invented by Dr Rudolph Diesel, is, by its very nature, far more suited to the rigours of commercial operation and is also able to be enlarged to give a greater power output than its petrol-fuelled, spark-ignition equivalent. This was already becoming obvious in the road transport field, as witness the fairly rapid change over from petrol to diesel in the bus and lorry business; and since railways need, if anything, even bigger engines for their normally heavier vehicles, it should

cause no real surprise that the truly successful application of internal combustion in the railway arena had to await the development of newer and more powerful diesel engines. But the transmission of power from engine to wheels was different.

In this regard, I have already noted (Chapter 3) that the basic vibration characteristics of railway vehicles are quite different from those of the road equivalent and that the various solutions to the problem of getting power to railway wheels were, at the time, less than perfect. Under the circumstances, it is hardly surprising that attention turned to the possibility of using 'state of the art' electric traction motor technology, by now well understood by railway engineers, combined with the ability of an internal combustion engine to produce electric power by the simple expedient of letting it drive a generator rather than the wheels — ie the basic principle behind the modern high powered diesel-electric locomotive. But, as might well be imagined, there was, inevitably, a practical snag, not least in the realm of the self-contained passenger-carrying vehicle where weight saving is paramount so as to achieve operational economy. Here, the fundamental dilemma was that an engine plus generator big enough to produce the power required was no lightweight item, be it fuelled by petrol or diesel fuel.

This factor was and is usually acceptable in the purely locomotive field and events were to show that the diesel was the better choice; but as far as the lightweight railcar was concerned, the future had to be with some better form of weight saving mechanical transmission if at all possible. This was far easier said than done in the 1930s, hence the Armstrong-Whitworth experiments.

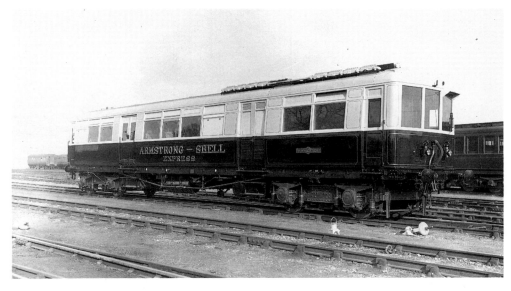

It began in 1931-2 with an undeniably well-conceived railcar design which bore more than a passing resemblance to the now familiar Sentinel offerings and with much the same capacity — 60 third class passengers in a 2 + 3 arrangement with 'reversible' seat backs. They were given 250HP Sulzer engines manufactured under licence and designed either to work in multiple or to handle an additional 30 ton trailing load at a designed maximum speed of 65mph. They were designed to a composite loading gauge enabling them to run anywhere in Britain; but they were rather heavy at 42½ tons. A very successful trial of two in multiple was carried out on the LNER in February 1932 from Newcastle to Hexham and back.

All told, three of these cars were built and their identity can be rather confusing. The first one (named *Tyneside Venturer* in 1932) appeared in late 1931 and this car ran in multiple with an un-named example on the 1932 Hexham trials. This second car, one of two built in 1932, was later named *Northumbrian*, but not until after it had undergone trials on the LMS (below). The other new car of 1932 was named *Lady Hamilton* later the same year and, along with the original *Tyneside Venturer*, remained on the LNER. The names are all believed to have been selected by the manufacturer and were certainly all applied to the outsides of the cars in association with the maker's blue and cream livery.

During 1933, the second car was evaluated by the LMS in a very different mode: a fast service from London to the British Industries Fair site at Castle Bromwich. This was the first diesel powered express service in Britain but by comparison with the LNER experiment, this operation, known as the 'Armstrong-Shell Express', seems to have been little more than an extravagant publicity stunt. The car was specially refurbished at Wolverton for the service and within the same body shell, the original 60 seats gave way to twelve Pullman-style chairs and tables, a small kitchen and pantry and separate toilet and lavatory compartments. No doubt it was all great fun but 42 tons of railcar for no more than a dozen passengers was no way to run

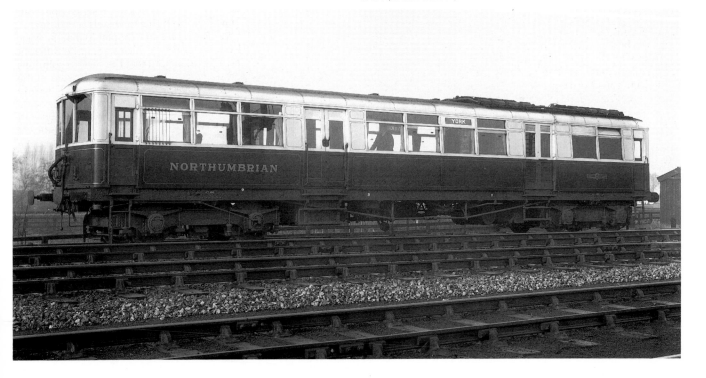

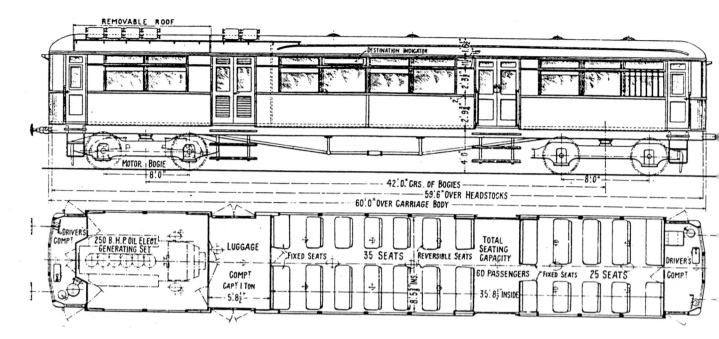

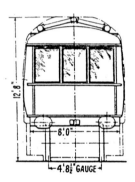

Contemporary drawing of the first Armstrong Whitworth diesel electric cars of 1931. This shows the normal interior seating arrangement. Scale: 3mm = 1ft

a railway, then or now! It was later transferred back to the LNER, reverting to a more practical high density seating arrangement, and had become *Northumbrian* by 1934.

At first, none of these cars belonged to the railways which tried them out but the LNER eventually purchased all three, *Tyneside Venturer* in 1932 and the other two in 1934. At first they had carried distinctive blue and cream liveries applied by their makers, but they were repainted into standard LNER green and cream railcar style some two years after their absorption by the LNER. For most of their working life, they fulfilled similar tasks to those of the Sentinels. Interestingly, amongst its duties, *Northumbrian* was operated within the York-Leeds-Harrogate triangle from 1934 and like the BR 'Pacer' cars some 50 years later (see previous chapter) was instrumental in increasing traffic. But like the steam railcars, this upsurge in trade could only be catered for by substituting more conventional trains. There was little in reserve and not enough railcars existed to increase the service frequency to anything like that seen today.

Unfortunately, in spite of their qualified success, increasing unreliability caused them all to be withdrawn in 1939.

The last Armstrong-Whitworth experiment is probably less well known than the previous example, but from the description given at the time, ought to have been a real challenger for honours. It appeared in 1933 and was an extremely well thought out 57 seater with compact underfloor diesel-electric equipment. Two engine options were stated to be available, either 95BHP or 140BHP, the whole lot coming out at something over 17½ tons with smaller engine or slightly under 19 tons with the larger, both being less than half that of the 1931-2 cars. The smaller engine was adopted from the outset — perhaps unfortunately in view of its later experiences (below). Regarded as a railbus, it had attractive bodywork by Park

Royal, the well known London bus builders and, like so many more of these things at the time, was tried out in Northumberland and Durham by the LNER and later in the King's Cross area too.

The LNER took it into stock in 1934 and in 1935, it too lost its 'private' blue/cream livery in favour of LNER green/cream; but it never received a name. Sadly, after a year or so, this innovative machine began to suffer a series of irritating mechanical failures and in the event, became even more unreliable than any of the first three diesel-electrics. It too was withdrawn in 1939 and thus it was that yet another interesting experiment which had been carried out mostly on former NER territory came to little. However, the four cars between them are estimated to have achieved a total of 700,000 revenue miles over the five year 1934-8 period which, on short distance routes, represents quite a reasonable achievement.

The alternative seating arrangement of 'The Armstrong Shell Express', an idea which only lasted a few weeks — see text. Scale: 3mm = 1ft

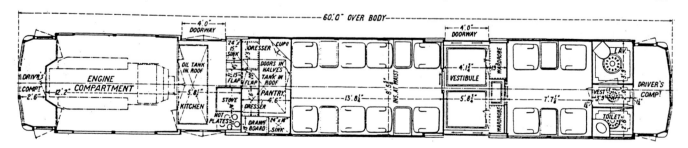

Lady Hamilton was the name given by Armstrong-Whitworth to the third of this interesting series of cars and is seen here in this official LNER view still in the makers' blue and cream colours which it received in mid-1932. Like Northumbrian, it ran in works grey for a time prior to that and was also purchased by the LNER in April 1934 after more trials in the Hull area, where it subsequently spent most of its time. It did not reveal its allocated LNER No.224 until repainted green and cream in August 1936 and after a period of intermittent reliability (like that of the others), it was marginally the last of the three to go, being withdrawn in December 1939. (LNER Official)

The early 1930s were interesting for the internal combustion engine as far as British railways were concerned, for they not only marked (more or less) the end of the experimental phase — including the various LMS ideas mentioned in Chapter 3 — but they also saw the start of the only development which had any significantly long-lasting consequences when, in 1933, the real way ahead was pointed by the first truly trend-setting designs to emerge during the grouping era. Interestingly, they embodied direct drive rather than traction motors and came from an unlikely source.

Tyneside Venturer was actually the first of the Armstrong-Whitworth diesel cars to appear, late in 1931, and by early 1932 had received its name and manufacturer's livery. Trials continued throughout 1932 when it was bought into LNER stock as No.25. As with the others, this number was not apparent until the car was repainted green and cream (November 1934) and it is seen here in this state at Scarborough on 16th August 1938. It was only a summer resident at the Yorkshire coast spa town, spending most of the rest of the year at Middlesbrough, albeit working regularly along the coast to Scarborough. During 1938 its reliability became ever more suspect and it was finally withdrawn in May 1939, following collision damage suffered at Middlesbrough a month earlier. (T. J. Edgington Collection)

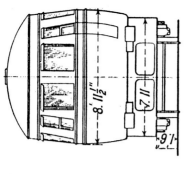

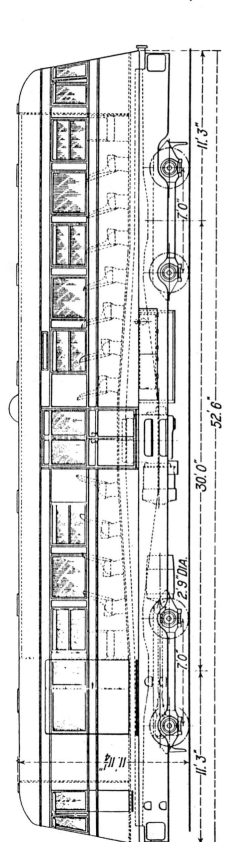

The Armstrong Whitworth diesel electric 'railbus' of 1933 with Park Royal bodywork. Scale of main drawing: 4mm = 1ft

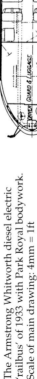

The nature of the fourth Armstrong-Whitworth diesel car (alternatively regarded as a rail bus) can be readily appreciated from this view taken at Newcastle in 1936 when it carried No.294 and green/cream livery. Like the three earlier examples, it began its life in Armstrong-Whitworth blue and cream and was also on loan for a time before being bought by the LNER in August 1934. It spent most of its time at Heaton though originally serving duty as standby for both Tyneside Venturer *and* Lady Hamilton *(in turn) from 1934 to 1936. It was not, in the event, even as reliable as the other three Armstrong-Whitworth cars and though at one time in 1937 seen as a possible replacement for the 'Bollington Bug' (Chapter 3) it was actually to become the first of the four Armstrong-Whitworth diesels to be taken out of service, in February 1939.* (T. J. Edgington Collection)

I refer, of course, to the pioneering diesel railcars of the Great Western Railway, by quite a long way the most properly integrated internal combustion railway passenger vehicles so far seen in this country. In them could be seen not only a proper appreciation of the different needs of a railway as opposed to a road vehicle but also a properly designed form of mechanical transmission which took care of the technical problems mentioned previously, not least that of humping a heavy generator around at the expense of extra passenger capacity. They were also more than normally well styled, being entirely appropriate to their era, yet having a timeless quality which does not always go with being in the height of fashion. Fortunately, they have attracted their own dedicated literature so it is not necessary to pick their bones here. What is maybe most surprising is that in spite of their longer term influence, there were less than 40 of them all told.

Their detailed story, as with that of the Sentinel steam railcars (Chapter 4), is very well recorded in terms of technology, appearance and other like matters — again see Bibliography — but since these fine surveys do not really 'place' them in relation to developments in the broader field with which this survey is primarily concerned, no apology is offered for giving them the rather more than brief mention which might otherwise suffice. They were important.

The story started modestly enough in 1933 when a new design of diesel-powered railcar was designed by Hardy Motors Ltd. of Southall, in association with Messrs AEC Ltd. (who provided the 130 HP power plant) and the GWR which agreed to operate the car on its services between Slough, Reading, Didcot and Oxford. A notably handsome and fully streamlined car body was evolved in wind tunnel tests and put together by Park Royal Coachworks Ltd. There was thus a very considerable injection of contemporary road vehicle technology; but where the idea differed from previous attempts to marry road to rail was in the exact use of the diesel engine itself.

This was achieved by incorporating it with a more robust chassis suitable to railway use, thereby allowing a form of direct drive transmission to be provided which was not only reliable but also capable of operating with equal facility in either direction of travel, the car being double-ended. When it finally emerged, it was a stylistic tour de force whose appearance met with immediate approval and brought the GWR much kudos. Though the company itself had little or nothing to do with its design, it was perfectly entitled to take credit for having introduced the car onto its routes.

After considerable evaluation, the GWR ordered a further series of cars which embodied improvements on the prototype, not least being the provision of twin engines for much needed greater power — the only real shortcoming in the earlier car. By 1936, no fewer than seventeen were in service which, though all sharing the basic streamlined shape of the prototype, albeit fine-tuned to a degree, were by no means identical, either in appearance or seating capacity.

The first 'production' series (Nos.2-4) of 1934 were low capacity, 44 seat cars for longer distance work, each having lavatories together with a small but well equipped buffet section at one end. Destined for 'express' service between Cardiff and Birmingham, they represented the first regular diesel workings in Britain of this kind, the earlier Armstrong-Whitworth car (above) having been essentially a one-off. Seats were

The first production series of GWR diesel railcars was for long distance work and appeared in 1934 — see text. The last of them, No.4, built in mid-September 1934, is seen here at Swindon on 20th March 1960, immediately after restoration following the decision to preserve it in the National collection when it was withdrawn from service in July 1958. It was further refurbished after the formation of the NRM and may still be seen at the Swindon museum. (T. J. Edgington)

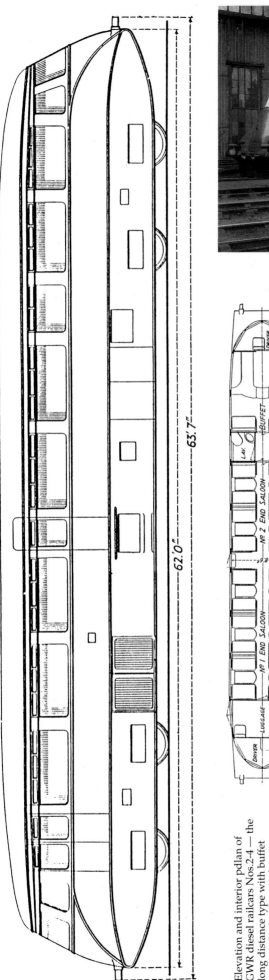

Elevation and interior plan of GWR diesel railcars Nos.2-4 — the long distance type with buffet counter. Scale of main drawing: 4mm = 1ft

arranged 2 + 2 in bays of eight with tables between them (as in conventional open stock) and a pair of centre doors was provided, one each side. The driver gained access to his cab from the passenger saloon, unlike Car No.1 where there was an outer door to the cab, and there was a small guard's and luggage compartment at the end opposite the buffet counter.

Happily, Car No.4 of this trio is quite properly preserved in the National Collection and currently (1995), may be seen at Swindon, albeit in non-working configuration. The writer can lay some claim to having been responsible for its current cosmetic state of presentation when he worked at the National Railway Museum, although he was unsuccessful in arguing the case for having it restored to working order. Its importance is such that it really deserves to be displayed in the main collection alongside *Mallard* and the rest and I believe that it far better justifies a place at York than some historically unimportant trivia for which valuable space has been provided!

The next three cars (Nos.5-7) reverted to the high density seating of No.1, but the bodywork was made by Gloucester R.C.& W. Co. Ltd. and differently styled in that the side windows were much deeper, thus improving the outlook, while the centre doors were of the sliding type. The waist line was slightly upswept at the driving ends which, allied to the two-tone colour scheme, gave them a slightly boat-like appearance. The roof line also curved down slightly more over the cab ends and the effect of both these small style changes was to result in a most charming variant from the original rather high-waisted appearance of the first four. This low-waisted style remained the standard for the rest of the streamlined series, whose bodies were also built by the Gloucester company.

The last ten streamlined cars (Nos.8-17) were ordered before the previous batch were all in service, such was the faith of the GWR, and all were similar in lines to Nos.5-7, save that the waist line was now horizontal rather than upswept at the ends. Of these ten, six were exactly as Nos.5-7: ie 70-seaters with no lavatories; three (Nos.10-12) had lavatories for the longer distance work (but no buffet) and seated 63 in consequence, still in 3 + 2 configuration; while the last, No.17, was a dedicated express parcels car whose purpose was to speed up local passenger services in the London area essentially by taking over all the 'pick-up' parcels traffic which hitherto had caused extended stops to be made by many local trains. This experiment clearly proved successful; whether it needed to be streamlined to do the job is rather conjectural. . .

The first three low-waisted GWR railcars, built in 1935, sported a rather attractive up-swept appearance below the driver's windows, well shown in this picture of No.7 taken at Worcester Shrub Hill, c.1939 and working the Hereford to Oxford service while LMS Class 2P 4-4-0 No.529 shunts empty carriage stock The car was withdrawn in January 1959. (NRM Collection)

By mid-1936, therefore, the GWR had put a fleet of 16 passenger carrying cars into service and such was their success that the company could claim later the same year that it was operating them on something like 20% of its network and they were putting up over 1,000,000 miles per year — a 'per car per year' mileage approximating twice that achieved on the LNER by the above-mentioned Armstrong Whitworth diesel-electrics, itself no mean figure.

The lines on which they were operated are shown in the appended map and it was claimed that the services concerned represented about 2-3% of the GWR passenger mileage, most of which was extra business since, at that time, the railcars were supplementing existing schedules. In some cases they drummed up so much new business that conventional trains had to be substituted. This seems undoubtedly to have been the reason why, in 1937, the GWR put an experimental new car into service, No.18. This, while still semi-streamlined, lost some of the graceful lines of the earlier cars and was given railway pattern buffing and draw gear, the purpose being to evaluate whether it could haul a trailing load and still give the same or similar performance to single unit cars. It was given a much stronger underframe in consequence and geared differently; it more than exceeded expectations and from it stemmed the final GWR railcar types.

One obvious difference between No.18 and its predecessors was the larger luggage van portion, the latter also containing a steam heating boiler for use when a trailer was in tow. In consequence, seating was reduced to 49, still 3 + 2 and arranged in five bays, one seat being 'lost' at the central door to the van portion. However, the loss in seating capacity was deemed to be acceptable in view of the ability to pull a trailer since the larger van space would serve both components. This, accordingly, was made the basis for the next main 'build', Nos.19-33. This time, however the bodies were built at Swindon and they emerged during the early war years in 1940 and 1941.

The first low-waisted GWR railcars, Nos.5-7. Scale: 3mm = 1ft

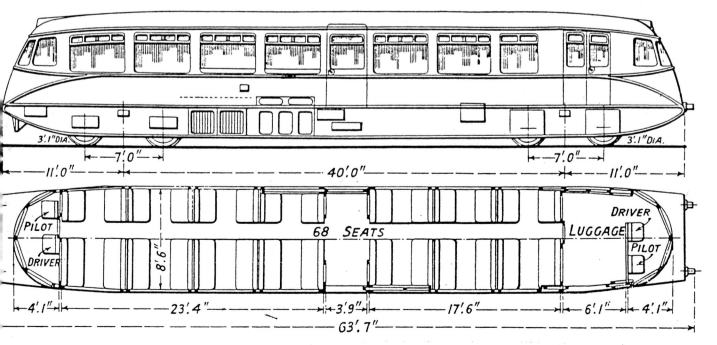

To those who had seen the earlier railcars, the new Swindon cars were a bit of a culture shock, being brutish in appearance with angular bodies and little real resemblance to their stylish forbears. They seemed all angles and corners in consequence; but this undoubtedly saved cost and time at a difficult period and in all other respects, they were more versatile because of their trailer-hauling capability. Inside, seating reverted to 2 + 2 throughout and they had six bays, still with a pretty large van and steam generator compartment. A final car to this same general outline was built in 1941: another dedicated parcels railcar in the manner of No.17 (above). Fortuitously, two of the main passenger carrying examples of this series (Nos.20/22) also survive in private preservation: at Didcot and on the Kent & East Sussex line.

After the building of this final tranche of single unit cars, it was not very long before the obvious next step was taken of making a twin railcar unit to cope with bigger loads and the final phase saw two of these pairs produced, one each in 1941 and 1942: Nos.35/36 and 37/38. They were well-appointed cars with driving cabs at the outer ends only, together seating 104. They also had a well equipped buffet counter and the first pair replaced the original Nos.2-4 on the Cardiff-Birmingham run. Like the 19-33 series, these twins were designed to take an auxiliary trailer, this time marshalled between the two components; an ordinary corridor third was used for this purpose but at no time does the GWR seem to have contemplated designing a purpose-built matching trailer, though one was sketched out (but never built) for Car No.18 in 1936.

It was perhaps surprising that this final series of 'angular' cars, whether singles or twins, was actually allowed to go ahead early in the war, and because of their timing into service, their early utilisation is mostly obscured, largely in consequence of the clamp down on information. However, what can be said is that in them, the GWR had fairly accurately predicted quite a number of aspects which would be copied in the BR DMUs of the mid-1950s and later, in particular the twin forma-

No.W14W again, this time seen on a Stephenson Locomotive Society special working to former Cambrian Railways territory. Taken at Welshpool on 26th June 1956, the low level view gives a fine impression of both the nose-end styling of the low-waisted railcars and the quadruple cluster of horns set low at the front end. (T. J. Edgington)

tion. In some areas the GWR versions were actually better (the buffets for example). Furthermore, the cars themselves, unlike almost all other non-electric self-propelled stock from the company period, mostly enjoyed a near-normal length service life, the last of them not being withdrawn until late 1962. On all counts, though but few in number, they can perhaps be regarded as the most significant company contribution in this particular field.

The only other contender for longer standing influence in the diesel arena is the final project to be considered in this account: a fairly spectacular one-off experimental train introduced by the LMS in 1938; its long-term development and possible evolution, like so many other things, were both cut short by the war. The project took the form of a triple articulated railcar set driven by no fewer than six 125HP diesel engines, the drive being of the hydraulic pattern. Each engine drove a single axle and only the extreme outer axles of the unit were unpowered. The train was designed for multiple unit control, thus

Above: The last fully streamlined GWR railcar was dedicated parcels unit No.17, seen in this attractive view (probably posed for the occasion!) when newly in service during April 1936 and showing off the original GWR livery to perfection. It was intended for use in the London area and spent much time there, but was later moved to the Midlands — see next view — possibly in consequence of the arrival of the second dedicated parcels car, No.34, in 1941. It was a little lighter in tare weight than the passenger cars and had a carrying capacity of 10 tons. (Pendragon Collection)

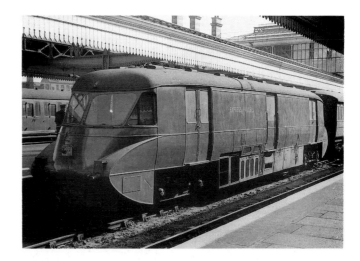

By 1955, the streamlined parcels car was BR No.W17W, lettered 'Express Parcels' and working out of Birmingham Snow Hill, where this picture was taken on 24th September. The livery was unlined crimson and the car must have had plenty of work, for it lasted just as long as the passenger types, not being withdrawn until January 1959. (T. J. Edgington)

The unique semi-streamlined car No.18, seen here outside Gloucester RC&W Works (which built the bodywork) in November 1936, went officially into service in April 1937. It had the same power unit as the earlier cars but was some four tons heavier by virtue of its much more substantial chassis and conventional drawgear. Designed to haul a tail load of up to 60 tons, it became the basis from which the final group of GWR cars was evolved and was the last car in the first phase of GWR diesel railcar development. It was withdrawn in May 1957.

This official photograph of the first of the 1940 Swindon-built GWR cars, taken at York by the LNER in 1944, marked the occasion when Nos.6 and 19 were on loan and destined for trial use on local services in the Newcastle area. By now, the car had lost its original 'shirt button' insignia in favour of the heraldic emblem and GWR initials; but whether it received a full repaint during those austerity years is not known. It is certainly very smart so maybe the Great Western felt obliged to give it a good finish for publicity reasons. The car itself was taken out of service as No.W19W in February 1960. (LNER Official)

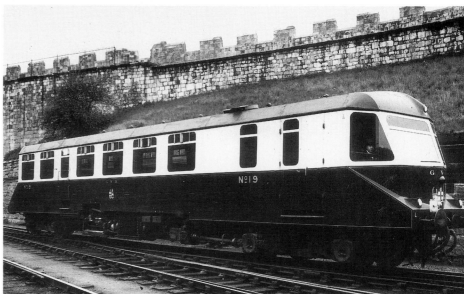

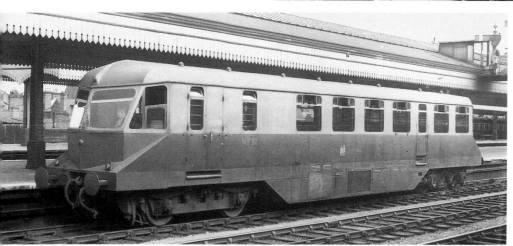

GWR No.32 was the penultimate single unit railcar and appeared in February 1941. It kept its GWR livery for quite some time, for it was still in its old company colours at Birmingham Snow Hill on a Dudley-Birmingham service on 29th July 1950. It was one of the last six survivors, all withdrawn simultaneously in October 1962. (T. J. Edgington)

At first, British Railways gave the crimson and cream livery to the GWR railcars which suited them far better than the multiple unit green with speed 'whiskers' which some of the longer-lived examples were to carry in their later days. This is No.W23W at Bristol, St Philips Marsh on 10th November 1957. Built in September 1940, this car too was one of the last six survivors — see previous view. (T. J. Edgington)

This undated view of the first of the twin railcars (Nos.35/6) was taken at an early date, for the GWR 'shirt button' emblem is just visible on the leading car and it has not yet acquired an intermediate trailer. Although these cars were designed to replace the original single unit cars on the Cardiff-Birmingham route, the traffic grew to such an extent that the twin cars had insufficient capacity (even with an extra trailer) and were found alternative work in the Reading and Bristol areas. Built in November 1941, this unit was officially withdrawn in April 1957, having been destroyed in a fire at Bristol a year earlier. (Pendragon Collection)

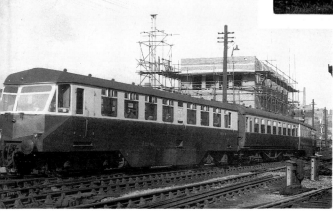

Towards the end of their lives, the GWR railcars were often requested for special enthusiast excursions and what eventually become the last twin unit to survive was photographed on such duty at Birmingham Snow Hill on 25th September 1954, the occasion being a Paddington to Towyn working in connection with the Talyllyn Railway Preservation Society. By now, the 'set' consisted of the original No.38 (built February 1942) and No.33, built in March 1941 as a double-ended car and replacing the original No.37 which had been damaged by fire in 1947 and withdrawn in 1949. From April 1948, No.22 in its original double ended form had replaced No.37 but in March 1954, No.33 was rebuilt to single ended form with gangway as a permanent replacement and remained with No.38 until both were withdrawn in August 1962. The unit is shown here with a conventional corridor third forming an auxiliary trailer between the two powered ends. (T. J. Edgington)

From the outside, the train was neatly streamlined with a very stylish end treatment, though maybe not quite so striking as that of the first GWR railcars. The cars themselves were built to conventional LMS practice (flush steel panels on timber frames) but underframes were centrally trussed in the manner of the LMS 1937 locomotive-hauled articulated stock. Given its length (184ft 6in) it was a commendably lightweight unit at 73 tons, more than one ton lighter than the GWR twins. The interiors were, if truth be told, more than a bit nondescript and apart from lavatories, there were no buffet or other refined facilities. It seated 162, of whom 24 were first class, while an interesting innovation was the provision of air-operated sliding doors. The seats, except where mounted against sides or bulkheads, were of reversible 'throw-over' type and it carried a quite spectacular new livery of Post Office red and ivory, topped by a 'silver' painted roof, the three tones being separated by black bands.

It is not quite clear what the LMS had in mind for this type of vehicle. Two-class accommodation put it one up on the one-class GWR cars but the lack of catering provision seemed to point the other way — ie outer suburban rather than true long distance. It was, therefore, rather surprising that after testing, it was put to work on the Midland main line from St Pancras as far as Leicester and Nottingham. It worked a complex six-service roster of 350 miles daily but little seems to have been recorded of its success or failure and it remained out of use during the war. Afterwards it was converted to a two-car maintenance unit for the MSJA electric line, losing four of its six engines in the process.

Whether or not the LMS form of transmission would have proved itself will never now be known but post-war events were to establish that for the most part, the hydraulic form was not usually the best way forward in British terms in any of its several modes of application and that the mechanical alternative was the best option for railcar use, even though the mechanical transmission adopted by BR was different in form from that of the GWR. Likewise, articulation was not to find any place in the BR solution whereas the GWR 'Twin' idea did. On the other hand, in terms of internal layout, though the LMS idea seems to have suffered from some confusion as to exact purpose, its two-class layout plus lavatories was very much the way that many early BR DMUs were set up.

making it the first genuine British DMU; but it never had a partner with which to work in multiple, even though one was planned. All power and transmission equipment was under-floor and the articulated bogies were of what was called the 'LMS type': a clever double pivot arrangement (one above each end of the bogies concerned) which allowed longer car units to be envisaged within the load gauge 'throw-over' limits than was possible with the more conventional Gresley-pattern centre pivot articulation. This allowed the outer ends to be some 64ft long.

This impressive LMS publicity shot was taken on the occasion of the launch of the LMS triple unit articulated railcar set in 1938. Why 'Patriot' Class 4-6-0 No.5507 Royal Tank Corps was chosen as the 'foil' is not known — maybe the LMS wanted a suitably older fashioned looking engine to contrast with the new look or perhaps it was just coincidence.
(LMS Official)

Perhaps it is reading too much into these final designs to try and trace any profound longer term influence on subsequent BR practice, for there were, in all conscience, very few of them anyway and the BR examples followed neither of them very closely. But of these last two pre-BR car designs, two things can be said. They both incorporated direct drive from engine to wheels rather than waste weight on electrical generating apparatus and however much or little they may have contributed to the post-war DMU scene, they did at least demonstrate, especially those of the GWR, that the long hoped for self-propelled passenger carrying unit was a realistic and practical possibility. Of this fact, BR took full advantage from the mid-1950s onwards and I venture to suggest that both the GWR and LMS examples offered not a few significant pointers on the way.

Amongst the first tasks of the LMS unit in 1938 were tests between Oxford and Bletchley. This undated view shows it at the former LNWR terminus of Oxford Rewley Road, where its ultra-modern lines must have looked very 'avant-garde' indeed in an environment which was otherwise almost wholly pre-group in nature.
(T. J. Edgington Collection)

Below:
By January 1939, when this official view was taken at Derby, the LMS unit had been slightly modified by way of receiving stone protection wires over the end windows and more substantial buffers — both features being shown here — and it is thought that it was in this form that it was operated on the old Midland main line — see text. There is, however, no obvious sign of conventional drawgear or the usual through carriage connections, though the unit was designed to run in multiple had the proposed second unit ever materialised.
(LMS Official)